# GOOD MOURNING CALIFORNIA

# GOOD MOURNING CALIFORNIA

# BARBARA STAUFFACHER SOLOMON

RIZZOLI
NEW YORK

First published in the United States of America in 1992
by Rizzoli International Publications, Inc.
300 Park Avenue South
New York, N.Y. 10010

Copyright © 1992
Rizzoli International Publications, Inc.

Library of Congress Cataloging-in-Publication Data

Solomon, Barbara Stauffacher
    Good mourning California / Barbara Stauffacher Solomon.
        p.   cm.
    Includes bibliographical references (p.   ).
    ISBN 0-8478-1541-2 (HC). — ISBN 0-8478-1542-0 (PBK)
    1. Landscape—California.   2. California—Description and travel.
    I. Title.
    F861.S68 1993
    917.94—dc20                                        91-39730
                                                          CIP


Photographs, drawings, and text by Barbara Stauffacher Solomon

Designed by Barbara Stauffacher Solomon
Printed and bound in Japan

# CONTENTS

Thank you
David Morton,
Paula Dietz,
Gunther Barth,
Amy Miller,
Ray Mondini,
June Oppen Degnan,
Johanna Schmidlin,
Rebecca Solnit,
Stanley Saitowitz,
Vito Acconci,
Richard Weinstein,
Kevin Starr,
Allen Temko,
Gary Strang,
Dawn Garcia,
Daniel Del Solar,
Sue Yung Li Ikeda,
Jeff Gundersen,
Gabriel Ruspini,
John Bass,
Chloe Stauffacher, and
Nellie King Solomon.

# GOOD MOURNING CALIFORNIA

This book is about *nature*, *gardens*, and *landscapes* in California. These three words, like California itself, have come to mean so many things that, though they are craved, they are avoided by careful people.

Why California? My parents were born here, I was born here, and for me swimming out into the Pacific is survival, not suicide.

In *Good Mourning California*, I am trying to catch California, suddenly, and for a moment. There are too many quotes, but I did not invent the myth of California. Everybody did.

The words and drawings were made consecutively, yet they are as contradictory as California. I talk about landscapes without frames, but each page is framed by the 8½" x 11" paper size and by my own limitations. If, between the covers of the book, there is a roller coaster, this is California.

The book ends with thirteen views of the landscape. There could be as many as there are people who have been seduced by some lines on a map promising paradise.

Calafía: the Queen of California.

9

## The Island of California

When I looked up California in *The Dictionary of Imaginary Places*, I was surprised to find it was not there. But it was in Garcia Ordòñez de Montalvo's 1510 Spanish romance *Las sergas de Esplandian*:

"Know then, that, on the right hand of the Indies, there is an island called California, very close to the site of the Terrestrial Paradise, and it was peopled by black women . . . who lived in the fashion of Amazons. They were of strong and hardy bodies, of ardent courage and great force. Their island was the strongest in all the world with its steep cliffs and rocky shores. Their arms were all of gold, and so was the harness of the wild beasts which they tamed and rode. For, in the whole island, there was no metal but gold. . . .

There reigned in this island of California a Queen, very large in person, the most beautiful of all of them, of blooming years, and in her thoughts desirous of achieving great things, strong of limb, and of great courage, more than any of those who had filled her throne before her. . . .

When Queen Calafía and her women, armed with that armor of gold, all adorned with the most precious stones, which are to be found in the island of California like stones of the field for their abundance . . . [ventured out to] . . . the great fame which would be theirs in all the world . . . they caused so much injury . . . that it may cause you equal pleasure. . . .

Where the danger came, there the safety came also . . . "

California was named before it was known. It was invented as Paradise before it was found to be precarious. The actual "discovery" of a hostile desert at the end of the world did not properly predict that this piece of real estate would become "the total myth" of the twentieth century: misconception, or myth–conception, Montalvo's yellow-bound novel did.

Myths dictate destiny; myths make us move mountains.

When Columbus sailed west to the white margin on the left side of the piece of paper, he reported hearing about an island inhabited exclusively by women which he did not have time to visit. To ridicule Columbus's tale, Montaĺvo invented an island with Queen Calafía on the throne and gold in the ground; heroes and losers started out to find and make California.

An island is an image for the imagination; I-lands appeal to the ego; an eye–land makes an irresistible target. Promise a treasure island, give a clue, paint Paradise where everything you lost, or want to find, is found, where fear is forgotten and greed is allowed, and people will buy a ticket to the possible.

Until various romantics glorified the wilderness as sublime, it was the open unknown; blank wilderness was the white space on the map, drawn by omission, drawn incorrectly, or not drawn at all, but covered with text or angel faces blowing winds. Myth makers pictured seductive nymphs, not hostile natives; maps showed what you might get, not what you could lose. Maps make the invisible visible.

Draw a map; make a point, and another; draw a line between them and everybody will get on it and go. Maps precede places. Maps are colored lines and blobs, targets, that tell people what they do not know, and people will follow them anywhere. Each squiggle draws someone's autobiography. The beauty of the drawing is not supposed to be important but it is not invisible. The same people who devise the myths draw up the maps. Princes and promoters, artists and admen, sorcerers and scientists promote seductive images, and people rush compulsively to a name or point on a piece of paper. Maps are drawings of unseeable landscapes, without people, which people use to see landscapes. Maps provide ways to get to islands like California.

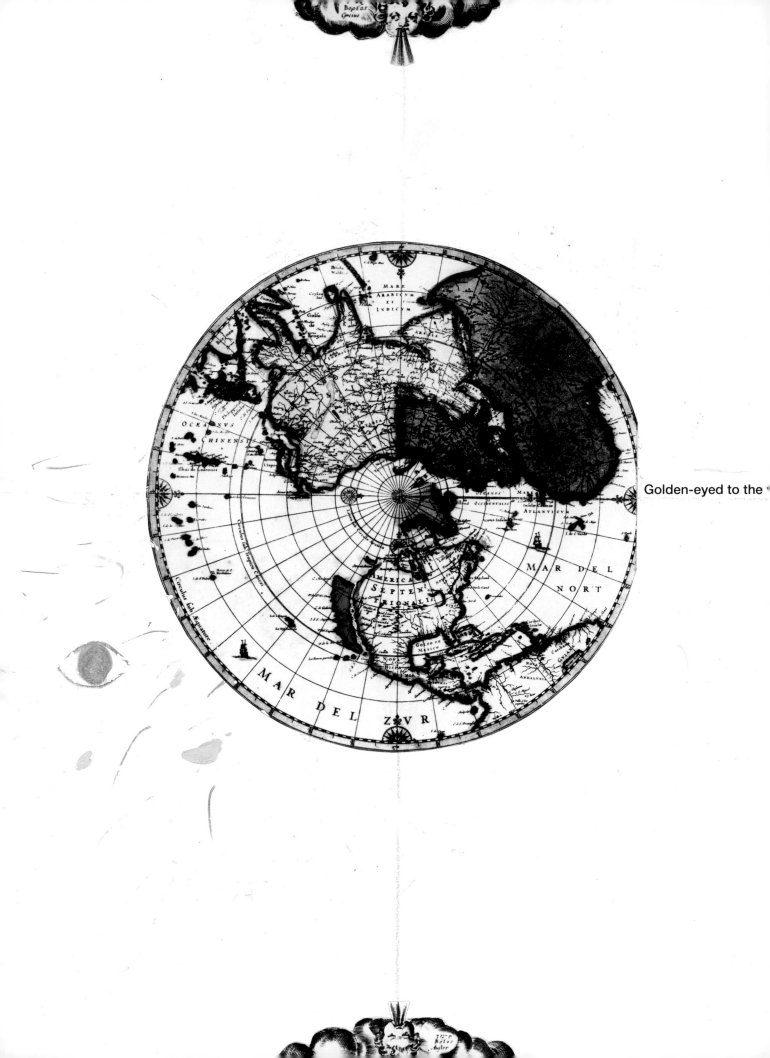

Golden-eyed to the

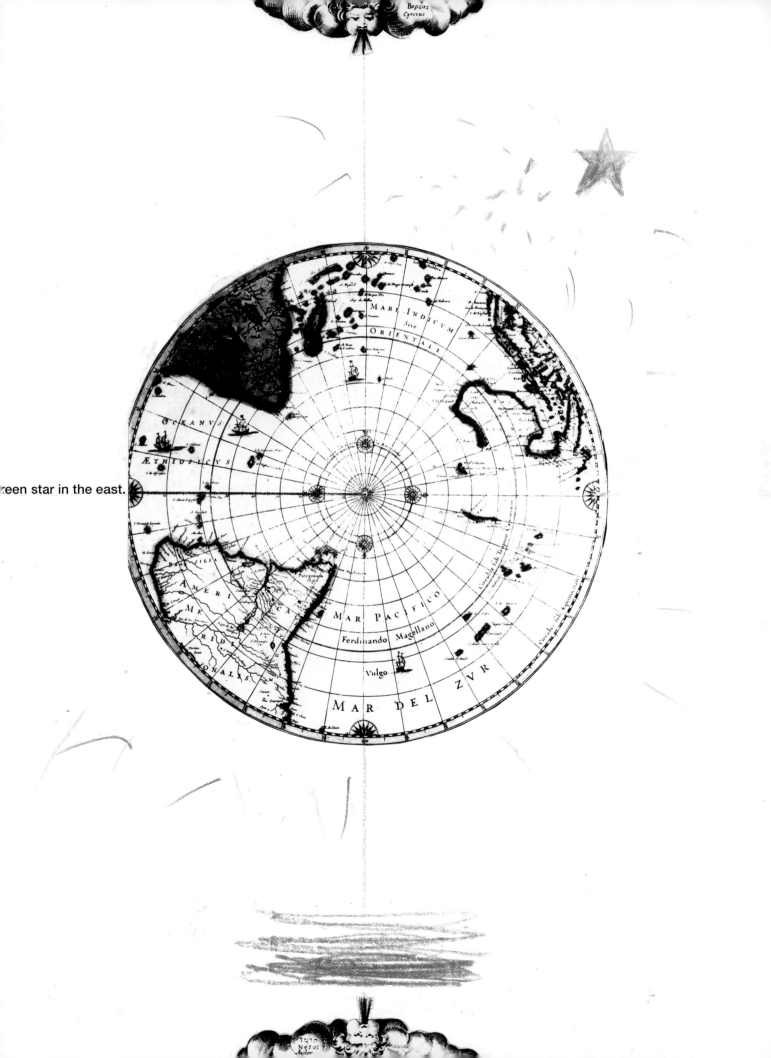

...een star in the east.

When the Spanish sailed into the white wilderness, they were looking for golden myths, for Paradise, for El Dorado, for the realm of La Gran Quivira with the Seven Cities of Cíbola, and for the legendary Strait of Anián leading straight to Asia.

In 1522, Hernán Cortés sailed from Mexico to discover the possible. The 1532 expedition, under Diego Hurtedo de Mendoza, was shipwrecked; the 1533 voyage ended with the murder of Captain Diego de Becerra by mutineer Fortún Jimenéz and the subsequent murder of Jimenéz by the natives. Cortés's 1535 attempt to colonize the inhospitable land was a failure. In disgust, disillusionment and high fantasy, Jimenéz and Cortés, familiar with the Queen Calafía story, called hell heaven and named their discovery "California."

People were easily convinced. Fray Antonio de la Ascension, a Carmelite friar, who sailed in 1602–03 with Sebastián Vizcaíno up the Gulf of California and along the Pacific Coast from Cabo San Luca to Cape Mendocino, declared himself a cosmographer and drew a map of California as a large island. Fray Antonio had heard Indian tales of Quivira and the Strait of Anián and knew the Spanish ambitions. While the official maps of the exploration, showing California as a peninsula, "disappeared," his map was sent to the king of Spain and the Council of the Indies "that they may learn of the magnitude and position of this great realm . . . to use it for revising and correcting the existing maps of the earth, since many things that are drawn on these with reference to this realm are very different from what they are ln fact." After all, he had been there.

Fray Antonio's map became Spain's secret weapon in the trade wars. Copies were pirated by real pirates. Various squiggles were changed to avoid plagiarism. Maps were revised and views altered.

Benito Arias Montano, in his 1571 map of the world for the polyglot Bible, seemed sure of one thing in North America: Ophir, the Biblical land of gold, was clearly named and placed (on the mainland, not the island) exactly where, inevitably, in 1848, gold was discovered in California.

Notwithstanding this accident of accuracy, the myth of California as an island was preferred and propagated.

In 1615, Juan de Iturbe, while searching for pearls in the Gulf of California for Nicolas de Cardona, announced that he had sailed around the Strait of Anián west to the Pacific, proving that "California is a very large island and not part of the continent."

Antonio Vásquez de Espinosa declared in his definitive work on Spanish America that "California is an island, and not continental, as it is represented on the maps made by the cosmographers."

Convinced, Henry Briggs, the English mathematician who invented logarithms to the base of ten, wrote his *Treatise of the Northwest Passage to the South Seas* (1612), encouraging the English predilection for islands and their fervor for finding a short route west to the East.

In the official 1642 *Atlas of the World*, printed in Amsterdam, Abrahm Goos engraved his version of the Fray Antonio map.

The French furthered the vogue of the *Ile de Californie* by adding four large islands and numerous small ones in the Vermilion, sometimes called the Mediterranean Sea, between California and the continent.

Finally, in 1700, dubious French cartographer Guillaume Delisle drew California as neither an island nor part of the mainland, but ambiguously as a vast site on the piece of paper with the name C A L I F O R N I E graphically spread in large type over all of what is now California.

In 1715, the German mapmaker Pierre Van der As printed two maps of America: one map pictured California as an island; the other showed California connected to the known world. His customers could take their choice. So can we.

In 1991 two geologists drew a map on which California appears as an island. The new theory says that Antarctica and America were once connected. Five hundred seventy million years ago, when Antarctica and Australia migrated south and the Pacific Ocean was formed, there existed a large island exactly were the Island of California used to be drawn.

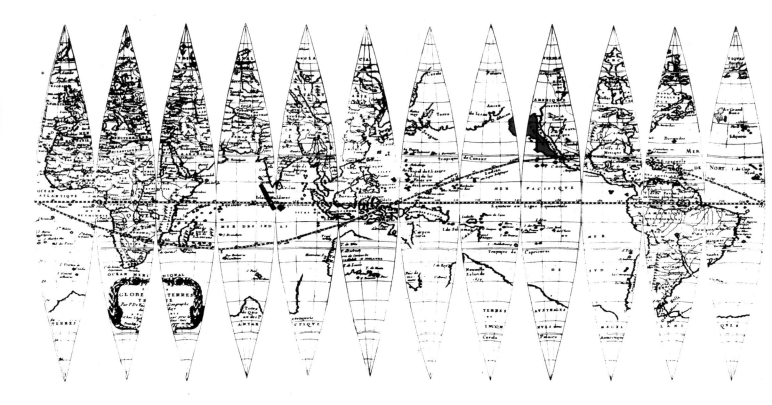

California: 1666.

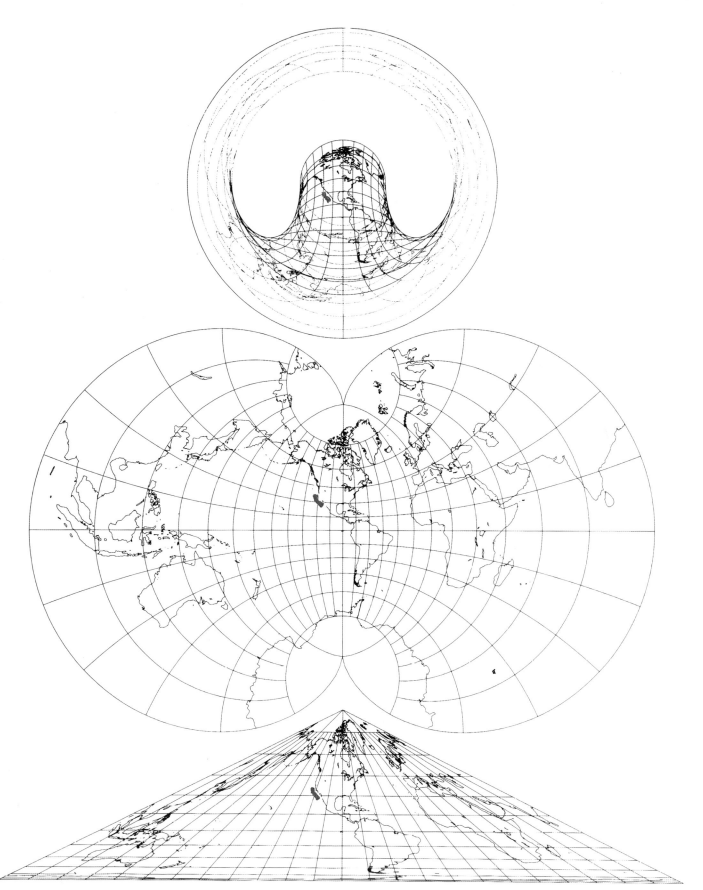

California: 1991.

# NATURE

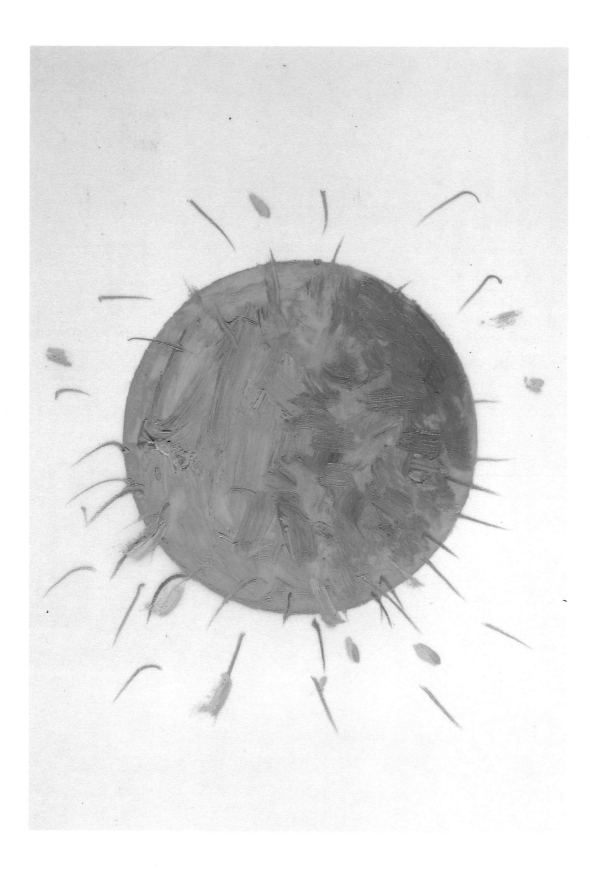

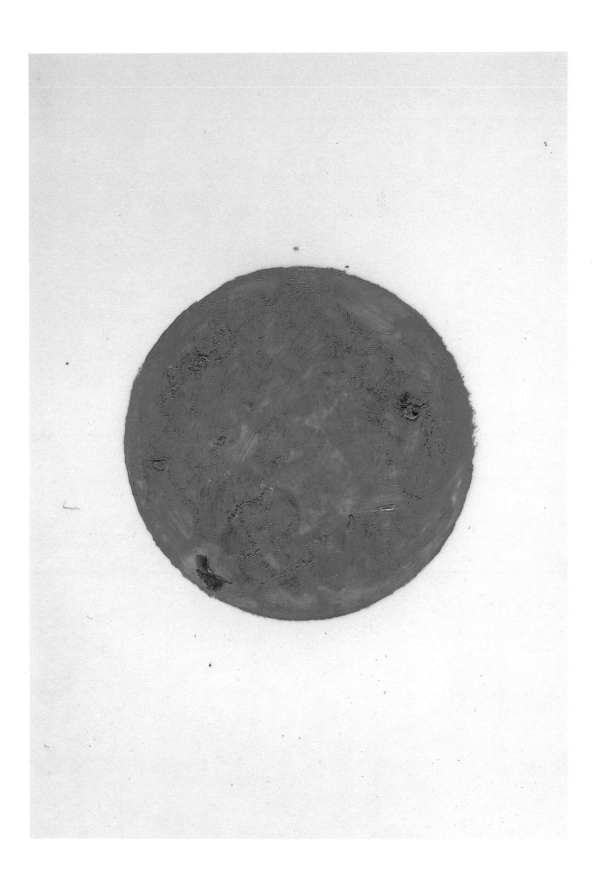

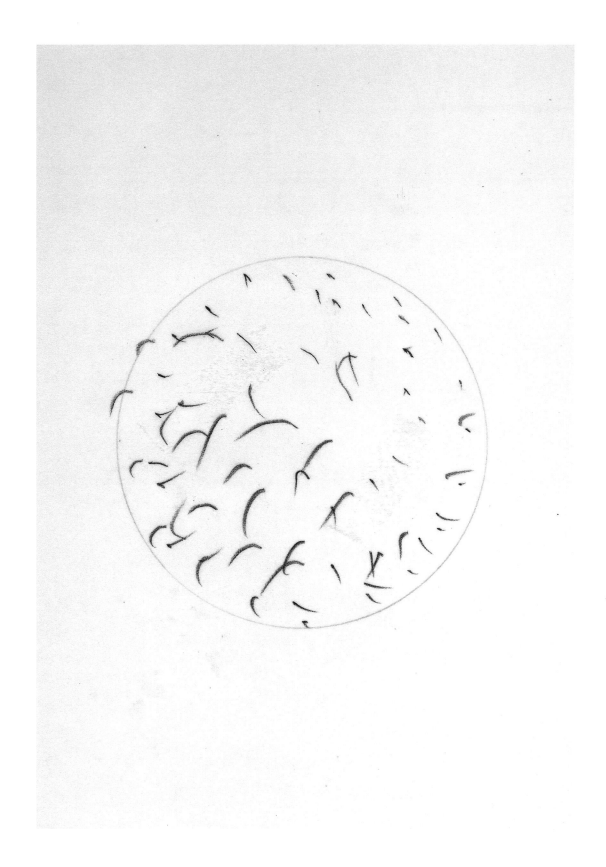

Nature, in California, is pure gold. Who can question myth when, "as if by design," gold was actually discovered here.

Consider the golden spectacles and commodities that nature offers in California:


The sun, golden, relentless, and blinding.
Crystalline light without shadow or memory,
so much light you can't see or think or hear.
Glaring views and phosphorescent fogs,
iridescent mists and fluorescent sunsets.
An immediate luminosity. Golden space.
Gold soil, desert dangers and dazzle,
bright white beaches, surf, and snow.
Yellow hills sparked up with orange poppies.
Even the giant trees are red. An aura of
expectation. Golden opportunities.
Golden women armored in gold and paint.

The Gold Rush, Fool's Gold, The Golden State,
gold fever, and The Girl of the Golden West.
"Eureka: I found it": the State motto.
"Oranges for Health; California for Wealth."
Sunkist labels, Sunmaiden, and Puregold juices.
Gold from the earth: yellow, green, and black.
"Oildorado in Eldorado." Acapulco Gold.
Tinseltown, Celluloid City, Lotusland,
gold stars born on the Silver Screen,
blond bombshells and platinum superstars,
Gold-wyn girls, Gold Cards, and glitter.
Marilyn Monroe as Earth Mother.

The yellow brick road to Paradise.
Yellow lines and dashes to Shangra-La-La-Lands.
Sunset Strip, film strips, and strip cities;
golden eyes from scrims, screens, and SIN-tilation;
klieg-eyes from kliegs, arc lights, and strobes.
Streets of gold made of neon and mirror glass.
Golden arches to Drive-In to. Glitz. Glamour.
Gold and Silver; the Reagan fashion colors.
Sunbelt suburbs, Orange County, Silicon Valley,
surfadelic natives, and xanthochroid sun-gods.
Electronic waves and fiber optic pixels.
Points of light chasing points of light.

San Francisco opening up her Golden Gate,
Los Angeles undulating before our eyes.

Nature, slippery, imagined, imaged,
shimmering emptiness, indifferent brilliance;
all gilt, no guilt.

Nature, like the Island of California, is imagination, and in California to imagine something is to make it happen, bigger and better. For Californians, nature is something that shakes us up, grows gold, and photographs splendidly.

In California nature has been seen as God, Mother Earth, Art, Inspiration, and Real Estate; it is the solar system, the star of every Western movie, a big swimming pool with one fish eating another, some of the worlds most expensive locations, a parking lot on the Pacific, and the Environment. Nature is what Californians build highways on in order to get out into nature. The latest trend is nature rediscovered and recycled as a scenic backdrop for beach houses, ski resorts, and National Park concessions. Nature in California has been imagined, coveted, conquered, used, misused, and used up.

**Nature in California is a myth:**

While some men made revolutions glued to the mountains of their homelands, others, more inspired or more desperate, heroes and losers, revolted with their feet and went to where the sun goes every evening. California was a nature myth waiting to be moved into.

Nature in the Far West did not look like the primeval green forests of Europe or New England. When people arrived at the back of the sun, they did not know how to see a wilderness they could not put into words and had not yet figured out how to use. The unexpected was ugly, the unfamiliar frightening. Deserts, voids, rocks, and silences,

"any color but green," were called "revolting," "dreary," "barren and boring." Geologists had not yet provided reassuring words such as "buttes" and "mesas," "plateaus," and "canyons."

Nature followed art. Early explorers borrowed words and views from the English nature poets. They painted "word pictures" of the familiar. Predictably, travelers sought out "meadows of grass vividly green," mountains "romantically beautiful," piles of rock that looked like fairy-tale castle ruins, and streams of "picturesque outline." Nature became scenery.

To imagine something is to make it happen.

**Nature in California is God:**

"Who can look at nature and not see God?" (St. Hilary). Europe may have history and art, but if "the heavens declare the glory of God, and the firmament sheweth His handywork," it seemed a divine imperative to get to California to see the most glorious "footprints" of God.

The word *sublime,* like the color gold, proved remarkably pervasive. Edmund Burke's *Philosophical Inquiry into the Origin of our Ideas of the Sublime and the Beautiful* (1756) had provided ways to see the Swiss Alps and the English moors which were perfect for promoting the Western wilderness as divine. Passion dispelled reason. Mountains that inspired astonishment and horror became sublime; deserts that aroused terror were beautiful. To experience God's power in nature "it was only necessary to open your eyes."

Henceforth entrepreneurs published guidebooks telling tourists of the West's "sublime beauty and awful grandeur." This campaign soothed America's aesthetic insecurities and was good for the railway business. People were curious to see the unknown. Terror at the sight of a real wilderness became popular when *Illustrated Guidebook Vision* told us how to see the West as a Panorama of Wonders.

Even geologist Clarence King succumbed to superstition (and John Ruskin's "ever-recurrent myth making") as he climbed from the California desert to the top of Mount Whitney and found it "hard not to invest these great, dominating peaks with consciousness."

And Henry Miller, sitting high above the Big Sur, found California to be "the face of the earth as the Creator intended it to look."

Romantic writers preached nature as God's (our God's) land. The wilderness was seen as a promise of divine regeneration; and righteous degeneration, the provocative virgin/ prostrate prostitute, waiting to be taken and saved by men with eyes to see. And, for a while, the government was giving it away free.

**Nature as wilderness:**

Calling California a wilderness was a convenient way to will away the native civilization of about three hundred thousand people, their gods, and their names for every hill and tree and point on the land, each name a center of the world that we had no intention of acknowledging.

Nature as romantic wilderness is described, painted, and photographed as if the words, brushes, and camera buttons are pushed around by humming birds and eagles. Unfortunately, if we must have nature untouched by people and their equipment, there is none. If California wilderness has to be virgin, "she" isn't.

If we admit that nature is the whole apparition, we have to agree that people, with their always more clever paraphernalia, invent the myths, paint the wilderness paintings, and push the buttons.

**Nature for Californians:**

If we find it unendurable to forsake nature as wilderness, we can "Go West. . . ." to where the Pacific still looks like a blank sheet of paper on which to draw our dreams. People see the red light at the end of the line and STOP "to dance at the edge of the world."

For Californians, nature is the Pacific light that makes most ugly possibilities glorious. There is so much light that you can't see or remember what happened last Sunday. The white blaze washes people and history clean. People rush to the too bright sun, golden and demanding. They go blind. In California, the sun is the star that keeps us alive, and we still believe it circles around us.

The horizon seems straight, but it flickers, recedes, and is always out of sight; a continuous scrim, gold, green, and vast, from the bright surf to the sky. There is a clear view of nothing.

For people who have never been here: "Nature in California is a Hollywood parody of ancient Mediterranean landscapes; a sea that is too blue, mountains that are too rugged, a climate that is too gentle or too arid, and uninhabited disenchanted nature, deserted by the gods: sinister land beneath a sun that is too bright" (G. Faye).

California "makes God to be a moneyed gentleman who scatters a handful of pennies in order to see mankind scramble for them. Going to California. It is only three thousand miles nearer to hell" (Henry David Thoreau).

GOD

Mother Nature

**Nature in California is a commodity:**

"You get a sense of power from these wide views, a habit of personal independence from the contemplation of a world that the eyes seem to own"(Josiah Royce).

Contemplation was fast followed by expectation; owning nature with your eyes led, almost immediately, to owning it with Claim to Title.

The big "take-off" to physically straddle, and industrially consume, nature began about 1830. The romantic malleability of nature merged with the capitalist necessity to use it. Nature in the West was affiliated with nationalism: it was our Manifest Destiny to get our feet wet in the Pacific. California was the gold ring at the end of the ride; the final reward, the most spectacular display of geography by which to know ourselves.

When Ralph Waldo Emerson said "The kingdom of man over nature [is] a dominion such as now is beyond the dream of God. . . . Who can set bounds to the possibilities of man?" everyone agreed.

Emerson, the Transcendentalist, saw nature as spirit: "Standing on the bare ground—my head bathed by the blithe air and uplifted into infinite space—all mean egoism vanished. I become a transparent eyeball; I am nothing; I see all." whereas, Emerson, "the seer of laissez–faire capitalism" (Daniel Aaron), saw nature as commodity: in *Nature* (1836) he wrote, "Nature not fixed but fluid. Spirit alters, moulds, makes it. . . . Every spirit builds itself a house; and beyond its house, a world. . . . The world exists for you. . . . The field is at once [man's] floor, his work-yard, his play–ground, his garden, and his bed." Nature as spirit and the spirit of capitalism made a happy marriage in *American Romanticism and the Market Place* (Michael T. Gilmore).

Emerson advised *The Young American* (1844) artist who saw technology as ugly to attach "every artificial thing and violations of nature" to nature "by a deeper insight" that will dispose "easily" with disagreeable facts. Henceforth painters painted shiny black locomotives into their golden pastorals; the white smoke from factories rose and merged picturesquely with the clouds.

**Nature is an escape movie:**

Henry Thoreau rebelled. He squatted alone in a simplified green world at Walden Pond (owned by Emerson) to escape "the curse of trade." He craved the "tonic of wilderness" and wrote, "Westward I go free," but in his imagination and his own backyard: "Be a Columbus to whole new continents and worlds within you opening new channels, not to trade but of thought. . . . [E]xplore the private sea . . . the Pacific of being alone."

Thoreau made a modern myth of his personal experiences. His dilemma was life and/or art, making "the earth say beans instead of grass," and/or writing a script for his self-conscious home movie. Half-reading his words, young men, nature boys, acid heads, and EcoWarriors escape westward freely to emulate his nature trip and make their private movies.

**Nature in California is scenery:**

"Have you reckoned that landscape took substance and form that it might be painted as a picture?" (Walt Whitman).

Like sunsets over the Pacific and gold in the ground, Yosemite Valley was a fortuitous find for California's reputation and self-esteem. Snow colored the granite walls white in winter, rains watered the Tuolumme Meadows green each spring, and Albert Bierstadt arrived to paint God, golden, bright white and blond, in the center of the canvas. The wilderness reflected His spotlight on the horizon, luminous and beckoning.

God makes his special effects; we make ours.

Yosemite was waiting to have its portrait painted and Bierstadt was a master at painting myths. The timing of his skill with the West's urge for publicity was destiny. Bierstadt's art, like the West, was entrepreneurial, entertaining, and BIG. As special effects, Bierstadt's theatrical "Great Pictures" come somewhere between the past as a moving diorama and the future as Cinemascope. Mark Twain, who knew California, found Bierstadt's Yosemite "altogether too gorgeous . . . considerably more beautiful than the original . . . more the atmosphere of Kingdom-come than of California": exactly. According to a contemporary art critic, "He who lays his ear to the wild grass may perhaps hear the distant tramp, not of buffaloes, but of civilization, coming like an army" (*NY Leader,* 1864). To present golden views of Yosemite in 1863, as idyllic antidotes to the Civil War, only furthered the myth of an undefiled paradise.

**Nature in California is a wilderness theme park:**

In the 1860s Thomas Starr King, through his correct reading of nature's spiritual "hieroglyphic," tried to guide people toward "Yosemites of the soul." Yet, looking down into the valley, he felt speechless: "Is there such a ride possible in another part of the planet?"

John Muir arrived and found words:

"No pain here, no dull empty hours, no fear of the past, no fear of the future. These blessed mountains are so compactly filled with God's beauty, no petty personal hope or experience has room to be. Drinking this champagne water is pure pleasure, so is breathing the living air, and every movement of limbs is pleasure, while the whole body seems to feel beauty when exposed to it as it feels the campfire or sunshine, entering not by the eyes alone, but equally through all one's flesh like radiant heat, making a passionate ecstatic pleasure-glow not explainable. One's body then seems homogeneous throughout, sound as a crystal."

Muir fled his father's Midwestern backyard to enroll in "the University of the Wilderness"; he came to Yosemite "as if it were a garden." Drunk on mountains and moonbeams, he hiked into "the heart of the storm" to see nature "more plainly." Before writing about Yosemite Falls he plunged into "the raw quick flesh of the mountain" and curled up "like a young fern frond" on a ledge to enjoy a "thundering bath" in the freezing mist. Though Muir transcended the sublime through Emerson's transparent eyeball, he preferred movement to meditation: Muir became a Californian.

Emerson said, "If you go expressly to look at the moon, it becomes tinsel." Muir looked: everyone came. Yosemite was framed by transcendental rhetoric, sublime garden walls, and sold to to a hungry public. Yosemite is now YosemiteLand. Tickets for campsites are purchased by TeleTron. People arrive by the express bus to Yosemite from Chinatown and go on to Hearst's Castle and Disneyland. The "crown jewel" became a "cash cow" ravished by its own popularity. There is Old Inspiration Point, and a new Inspiration Point; inspiration in California is notoriously shifty.

**Nature in California is a photo opportunity:**

Nature usually benefits from primping and grooming. Artists and their audiences are hypnotized by illusions, retouched images, and any

Equestrian Statue on 395.

wilderness shot with bright horizons framed somewhere in the distance.

Bierstadt only traveled to California after he saw Carlton Watkins's "unbelievable" photographs of Yosemite, which were carefully conceived (he hauled the latest heavy equipment to the wildest vantage points) to look as much as possible like Bierstadt's "unbelievable" canvases. For his Yosemite landscapes Bierstadt made photographs and field sketches and then returned to his studio on 10th Street in New York to rearrange everything for effect, to paint Claude Lorrain pastorals in the foreground and popular pink-gold Salvator Rosa clouds in the sky.

For dramatic shots photographer Eadweard Muybridge played acrobat on treacherous ledges, acted landscape architect cutting down unsightly trees, and Cecil B. De Mille adding cloud effects in the darkroom. For the Pictorialists, more interested in the moods created by vaseline than geology, the framed film was their canvas and Ansel Adams achieved "Yosemite sublime" through the use of storms and dark red lenses.

Now that only three percent of the visiting tourist-photographers get more than one hundred yards from their cars, Yosemite Valley is a giant parking-lot-photo-op. Signs direct you to Scenic Points to help you aim your camera. When you get home you can have the film developed and see where you have been. Each time a camera clicks, Yosemite is framed and made more famous.

Since there is no more divine wilderness to pray in, we have California's divine ambience to play in. Since we no longer believe in the hypocrisy of transcendence, we can simply enjoy being bombarded by "the spectacle."

Walt Whitman's marching songs joyously rushed people west to remodel nature into the technological sublime. From "a single spear of grass . . . the journey work of the stars" Whitman fired up foundry chimneys with flaming lights projecting "masculine full-sized and golden" onto the landscape:

"Facing West from California . . . the shores of my Western sea the circle almost circled. . . . We debouch upon a newer mightier world. . . . Never was average man, his souls more energetic, more like a God; . . . he colonizes the Pacific, the archipelagoes; With the steam-ship, the electric telegraph, the newspaper . . . he interlinks all geography, all lands."

"Wake Up!" to nature winking, blinking, in the California landscape of images whizzing by to buy. The "circle [is] circled" now that the Japanese are buying "the shores of [our] Western sea."

"What thoughts I have of you tonight, Walt Whitman, for I walked down the side streets under the trees with a headache self-conscious looking at the full moon. In my hungry fatigue, and shopping for images I went into the neon fruit supermarket, dreaming of your enumerations" (Allen Ginsberg).

**Nature in California is *Dreams That Money Can Buy* (1946):**

In California, we remade nature to look the way the myths told us we wanted it to look. The new playgrounds are more tidy than the originals, and more accessible; everything is available, successful, and consumed.

**Nature in California is a supermarket:**

In our neon hunger to capitalize on California's surprising spectacles and golden commodities, we promptly package them for successful marketability. Supermarkets are utopia, the myth of the Golden Age, and *The Eclogues* of Virgil.

"Give me your sick and your dying and I will heal them with a one-time designer's close-out sale, this weekend only" (John Chase).

The sun is for sale in California.

The new Regional Shopping Centers are Treasure Islands surrounded by seas of PARKing, where the consumption of Mother Nature is seductively disguised as family entertainment.

The chrome-and-glass malls are our Crystal Cathedrals, civic centers, amusement parks, baby sitters, and paradise gardens. We can promenade up and down the always green *allées* choosing from every trend in diamond rings and cabbages, diets gadgets, cars, architecture, politics, and fantasies. There is a new perfume called CALIFORNIA: A great Way To Feel About Yourself. Hilltop Mall is best for story hour, but Fashion's Tilt on the Island has a better arcade. When mallwalkers get dazed from overexposure, they get mall-eyed. Everybody is playacting *My Life in the Mall*.

Nothing is free but freedom of choice. And escapism. The twenty-five-screen video wall flashes packaged messages from God, CNN, and MTV. History is available at the multi-mini-mall movie palaces. Geography comes with the exotic franchised fast-food facades. The Nature Store offers green walls of garden books and panoramic posters as facsimiles of wilderness nature lost and longed for. The Garden Center sells souvenir seedlings, packaged clean dirt, and squares of grass by the foot ready to lay out as instant nature decor.

Everything is astonishing and in abundance, here and now, in paradise, the Golden State.

At each shopping center, nature, the "gregarious mass world of objects," is accessible to our gaze. Each object is silent, waiting, as special as a fairy tale, displaying its "fresh from the assembly line" mythology. Every carefully designed and printed label is persistently facing flat-out to its eager audience. Yellow boxes are piled on yellow boxes, red cans on red cans, ordered into gridded walls of color. Since the 1960s, when pop artists taught us to wander through stores "as if they were museums" (Claes Oldenburg), every label and logo is capital carnival art.

In the Good Life and Real Food boutiques, each carefully arranged eggplant is an art object, each pyramid of oranges a sculpture. Selecting spices out of open bins is like choosing pigments for a masterpiece. We can stroll down the furrows plucking apples and artichokes and chops that don't remind us of dead lambs. Amber lights illuminate the tomatoes, green glows on the lettuce, and there are rainbow mists of pure water giving life to the vegetables. It's fashionable for peas to be packaged in pods again.

In California, supermarkets are SAFE-ways. Everything previously worshipped and desired in nature is improved upon. There is golden fruit without toil, flaws, or worms, in dizzying abundance, which everybody can buy and take home. It is nature perfected. The climate is always mild. It will not rain. Aerial music, the sounds of babbling brooks, and the song of whales are piped in. The dappled lighting is like sunlight in a forest. Time is erased. There are no seasons, or death. For twenty four hours, night and day, everything is available.

In California, nature is authentically synthetic: Paradise.

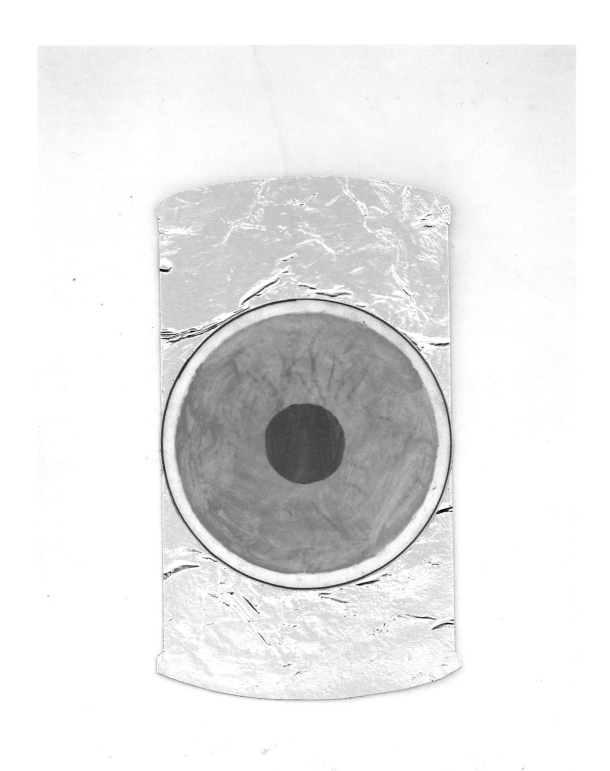

# GARDENS

In California the color *green*, like the word *nature*, is morally effective, politically useful, and economically profitable. Never mind that California is golden; if it is to be Eden, it has to be colored green.

Gardens are special locations that people dream about, buy, and have parties in. They are drawn up, planted, and expensive. They appear and disappear. Some are saved, picture perfect, in paintings, photographs, and glossy publications.

Gardens, like art and the movies, are framed images that people make and then move into. Gardens are enclosed by invisible fictions and visible walls; paintings end at their gilt frames or somewhere in the art world; movie plots move forward as each frame is framed by the fixed edge of the screen. To frame is to contrive a plan, to adjust things for a purpose, to limit the view "through the looking glass," to empower for a purpose, and to frame-up.

Frames give status to the fictions inside. Romping on your private lawn, working at a painting, and escaping into a movie are games played in special sanctuaries. Everybody wants to go to Eden, where eternal youth is promised and Eve is frolicking on the green grass.

If there was never a Garden of Eden, there is no California; it only appears to exist.

Eden was designed as an enclosed garden. Walls provided refuge from the wilderness outside. Inside, water, trees, and people were ordered. The words *garden* and *paradise* both come from roots meaning "enclosed." Four rivers divided Eden into four rectangles of green. When the rivers became paths, the straight, raked roads showed the proper conduct expected of good Christians. Monks cultivated their souls by nurturing plants in gardens called paradises; the Virgin Mary was described as paradise, a garden producing Christ, the Tree of Life, from her womb; and when Solomon married the black Queen Sheba, her enclosed garden was his paradise.

Since beaming up to Eden has been eliminated as a possibility, the search for an earthly substitute seems an obsession.

The Garden of Eden was where we came from. Much to our chagrin God threw us out. We had to make our own paradise to go to. And Californians want to have it all: a paradise that looks like Eden.

"In at least one respect California . . . resembles Eden; it is assumed that those who absent themselves from its blessings have been banished, exiled by some perversity of heart" (Joan Didion).

Praying or playing, people obey similar rigid rules, for a limited period of time, in ritualized sanctuaries or special playgrounds. The temple and the arena, the consecrated spot and the sports palace, the magic circle and the pool table, the court of justice and the tennis court are all isolated and particular, hallowed and hedged.

In California, rituals and games are played in the same gardens. Paint white lines on a fetish green lawn and everyone will follow the rules of the game. The lawn that hides the dead bodies is the same lawn that promises eternal life. Forest Lawn Cemetery is as popular for wedding parties as for funerals, and when the pope came to California, he headed straight for the biggest Astroturfed football stadiums to hold High Mass.

Hungry eyes feed on green grass: Coleridge's Xanadu colored by "sunny spots of greenery" and Wordsworth's "Splendors in the Grass." In *The Tempest* Shakespeare's magic isle, like Calafía's California, "indeed is tawny," but "How lush and lusty the grass looks! how green . . . With an eye of green in't." Artifice, and green-tinted glasses, "that art/Which you say adds to Nature, is an art/That Nature makes." Who does not envy green?

Green is the color of rebirth and resurrection: in "Walled-In Pond" (Thoreau's pun) the "Pond in Winter" is iced "vivid green . . . the color of the eyeball"; the grass "flames up on the hillside like a spring fire . . . not yellow but green is the color of its flame; the symbol of perpetual youth . . . So our human life but died down to its root, and still puts forth its green blade to eternity."

In *Leaves of Grass* Walt Whitman celebrates life by "observing a spear of summer grass." The child asks, "What is the grass?" and Whitman answers "it must be the flag of my disposition, out of hopeful green stuff woven./Or I guess it is the handkerchief of the Lord . . . the grass is itself a child . . . The smallest sprout shows there is really no death."

San Francisco is a city in the West where certain rectangles in the grid are colored green. We use them to perform rituals and play games, to improve our bodies and, incidentally, increase our chances of immortality.

San Francisco is almost an island and a garden: three sides are enclosed by water, the other by a wall of hills, still mostly unbuilt. As with most western towns, the ground is ordered by the Spanish grid of urban colonization prescribed by *The Law of the Indies*. Straight lines of streets are drawn, unrelentingly, from the Bay, up and down the hills, east and west, north and south, except for Market Street, a diagonal straight across town from the port into the cleavage of Twin Peaks. Even most freeways stop to bow politely to the grids as they enter the city. (Some that didn't were attacked by the 1989 earthquake and subsequently demolished.) Each residential block in the grid is zoned to enclose a smaller rectangle of green backyard within it. Golden Gate Park is a 1,017-acre green rectangle painted on the once-white sand dunes from the center of the city to the Pacific. Each green garden, park, and playground is particular, hallowed, and possessed, and San Franciscans obsessively play in their green rectangles of paradise: the map is drawn that way. San Francisco is planned for re-creation, tennis, and ping-pong.

Mr. Palomar's (Italo Calvino's) lawn is an "artificial object, composed of natural objects, namely grasses. The lawn's purpose is to represent nature, and this representation occurs as the substitution, for the nature proper to the area, of a nature in itself natural but artificial for this area. In other words, it costs money." Indeed, "seeing the lawn' is only an effect of our coarse and slapdash senses. . . ." for "the lawn is a collection of grasses . . . that includes a subcollection of cultivated grasses and a subcollection of spontaneous grasses known as weeds . . . and the wind blows . . . [and] . . . a lawn does not have precise boundaries" anyway.

Like any fiction claiming certitude, the myth that Eden is an orderly, enclosed garden alternates with the myth that the wilderness outside is the real paradise. Or, is it that romanticism was really born in the Garden of Eden and the serpent was the first romantic? Or was it Eve who just wanted to escape, to go west to California?

"A garden was the primitive prison, till man, with Promethean felicity and boldness, luckily sinned himself out of it" (Charles Lamb).

When we went west, out of the garden of civilization, toward the garden of the wilderness, the open spaces were hailed as potential paradises. Political romantics prescribed the cult of wilderness to purify the curses of civilization. God lived in trees, not in traffic. In 1893, when Frederick Jackson Turner proposed his then-revolutionary "frontier hypothesis" that American democracy was "born of free land," he contended that as long as there was free land available, ahead somewhere, each individual had the chance to move on to where he could cultivate his garden equal to any man. The problem with this myth was that as civilization moved across the wilderness, claiming, fencing, and mowing, we used up all the land that was supposed to make us free. When we hit the Pacific wall, we reverted to our usual civilized justifications for uncivilized exploitations.

Racism rules in the garden; in California, it always has. Visions turned into ambitions; landscapes became land speculation. Land rights linked with righteousness. And everybody white scorned everything brown. Protestants, eyeing and vying for Eden, had contempt for Catholic priests and Mexican landlords, "lax and lazy," with "nature doing everything and man doing nothing" (Sir George Simpson). "American Liberty vs. Mexican Tyranny": nature was affiliated with nationalism and justified racism. The blond gods painted the earth white, gold, and green; it was the Yankee's mission to make the golden desert bloom into a green English garden.

"Railway iron is a magician's rod in its power to evoke the sleeping energies of land and water" (Emerson). When Pullman provided luxurious drawing rooms speeding through the wastelands, the wilderness whizzed by, dreamlike, moving movies, cowboy scenery seemingly painted on glass. It became fashionable to ride in comfort in these long black boxes through the landscape. "Nothing improves scenery like ham and eggs" (Mark Twain). Heaven was sitting safe, up above the two precise stripes of black iron, at once parallel and converging into an inverted V, disappearing into the future in California pointing to paradise and profits in the "Pacific Eden."

"The entrance to California is to the tourist as wonderful and charming as though it were the gate to a veritable fairy-tale" (Charles Nordhoff, 1872). "At every turn we could see farther into the land and our own happy futures. . . . For this was indeed our destination; this was the 'good country' we had been going to so long" (Robert Louis Stevenson, 1879). Now you enter through a turnstile from Mexico as if somebody wants you to realize immediately that you are in an amusement park.

In California gardens are plots from somebody else's story.

In *The Wonderful Wizard of Oz* (1900) Midwestern author L. Frank Baum fantasized about Oz as "a material dream." When he moved to Coronado and then to Hollywood a few years later, Oz became a documentary. *The Marvelous Land of Oz* (1905) was "brim full of the sunshine of California; . . . a country of marvelous beauty. There were lovely patches of green sward all about, with stately trees bearing rich and luscious fruits." Oz is the "Garden of the West." Magically Oz-topia became a tidy, prosperous, and progressive Los Angeles, the greenback Emerald City of Angels. Pay no attention to the Wizard behind the curtain, just do as he says and put on your emerald-tinted glasses. Oz, and California, are a matter of how you look at them.

In the movie *The Wizard of Oz* (1939), MGM's Oz is "Somewhere over the Rainbow," the original "road movie," a paradise/wilderness garden (you get it both ways), and a rite-of-passage leading to an urban center celebrating the technological sublime. The road involves encounters with good and bad witches, phony green lawns, technicolor flowers, and assorted astonishing terrors. Though Kansas is black-and-white, everybody seems to want to return there.

Was California created to be a movie set?

In California the sun shines to light up the stars, nature is a fashionable commodity, and everybody escapes, blithely and continuously, into the flickering shadows dancing on the wall.

Hollywood, the myth capital of the twentieth century, quite appropriately, does not exist. Cahuenga Valley (Hollywood's name when people raised sheep there) was the site of the Cahuenga Capitulation of 1847, where Captain John Frémont, costumed as an the Old Californio, cynically charmed General Andrés Pico into ending the war (that the Yankees were illegally making against the Mexicans with whom the United States was supposed to be at peace) and took the land.

The actual location of Hollywood was a rose garden, built in 1901 by Paul De Longpre, a popular French painter of flower arrangements, at the end of the electric trolley line to Hollywood Boulevard. The spectacular garden and Moorish-style villa attracted tourists, and the creative eye of D. W. Griffith. Griffith rented the garden as a setting for *Love Among the Roses* (1910). Both plots grew simultaneously, the garden and the movie.

After the movie cameras focused on sex and splendor growing golden myths, and green money, in the rose garden, California became Eden on the back lot. Local landscapes were destroyed and, at the same time, made immortal; each detail preserved as shadows in cans. Reruns make us familiar with every curb cut in front of the Hollywood banks held up by movie gangsters on Sundays; light comedies show us how to act at Beverly Hills garden parties; the Keystone Kops taught everyone how to drive fast and ignore stop signs in California. "My childhood hometown was a piece of L.A. on the screen" (anonymous).

Landscapes at hand became international dreamlands. Built for *Intolerance* (1916), Griffith's Babylon, a three-hundred-foot monument of stairways and elephant gods made of papier-maché and bubble gum at Sunset and Hollywood boulevards, became a dreamscape for movie audiences and a historic monument for future Southern California architects to emulate. The fast schedules necessitated quick fixes and false fronts.

"Under the moon the back lot was thirty acres of fairyland—not because the location really looked like African jungles and French chateaux and schooners at anchor and Broadway at night, but because they looked like the torn picture books of childhood, like fragments of stories dancing in the open firelight" (F. Scott Fitzgerald).

The forgeries looked real and the real landscapes looked like forgeries: *Top Hat* (1935), *The Garden of Allah* (1936), *Lost Horizon* (1937), *The Adventures of Robin Hood* (1938), and *Casablanca* (1942) were all shot 'on location' in and around Hollywood. "There's Paramount's Paris, and Metro's Paris and, of course, Paris, France. Paramount's is the most Parisian" (Ernest Lubitsch).

Hollywood movie landscapes are a geography everyone shares. Before jets and satellites, these framed flashes of light at twenty-four frames per second were canned and projected onto blank waiting walls to be discovered and consumed by everybody rushing into the darkness to see the light. Each Hollywood shadow on the wall, in front of which "we deceptively thought we were only spectators, is the story of our life" (Italo Calvino).

For Europeans, California was a European invention. Emigrés arrived and took over the Hollywood myth business. They excelled in making fantasies as fantastic as their getting here in the first place. California was made accordingly into a house of (post)cards to send back home. Young Californians—moviemakers, writers, and designers—culturally insecure, were fascinated and flattered by the attention from older Europeans and influenced by their imported theories and techniques. The exiles basked in the native naïveté, the sun, and landscapes that looked to them like exotic surrealist scenery.

Myths of the West are made in Hollywood; golden opportunities, free individuals, free sex in the sunshine, and happy endings are known by everybody who sees westerns; and everybody does. Whether the mountains are shot on location, painted in the back lot, or modeled by special effects and computers, when the frames are seamlessly spliced together, we believe. In cowboy movies the scenery is a star of the show. You can't have westerns without the West.

John Ford's Myth of the Garden juxtaposes civilization progressing against, and over, the seductions of the Myth of the Wilderness. In *My Darling Clementine* (1946), the wild cowboy, Wyatt Earp, is civilized by the perfume of honeysuckle in the barber shop and the scent of marriage in the garden. In *The Man Who Shot Liberty Valance* (1962), the ordered Eden versus wanton wilderness conflict is introduced by an image of a cactus rose. When Senator Stoddard gets funds from Washington to build a dam in order to irrigate the desert and grow real roses, we know the cultivated garden is the winner and the hero. The Wild West is lauded, then promptly mowed into a lawn.

In *Shane* (1955), the hero remains free. Rufe Riker, the "bad" cattleman, maintains "We made this country. We found it and we made it"; Joe Stark, the "good" familyman farmer, prefers to cultivate his fenced garden. Shane appears mysteriously out of the wilderness, enters the plot, uses righteous gunplay for Joe's side of the argument but, in the end, hits the road again for nowhere. The winning of the West is the winning of the myth, and in Westerns, we get as true a "hi-story" as most of us will ever know.

In *Blade Runner* (1982) the space cowboy zooms from the apocalyptic black streets of Los Angeles in 2019 toward a green pastoral somewhere "off-world." The garden/wilderness choice is recycled in George Lucas's outerspace/Western Oz/odyssey *Star Wars* (1977) and in David Lynch's *Wild at Heart* (1990). In *Thelma and Louise* (1991) home is hell; on the road the people are not great, but the landscape is superb. Gradually, driving west through the open wilderness, nature offers freedom, liberation, and finally, ultimate transcendence.

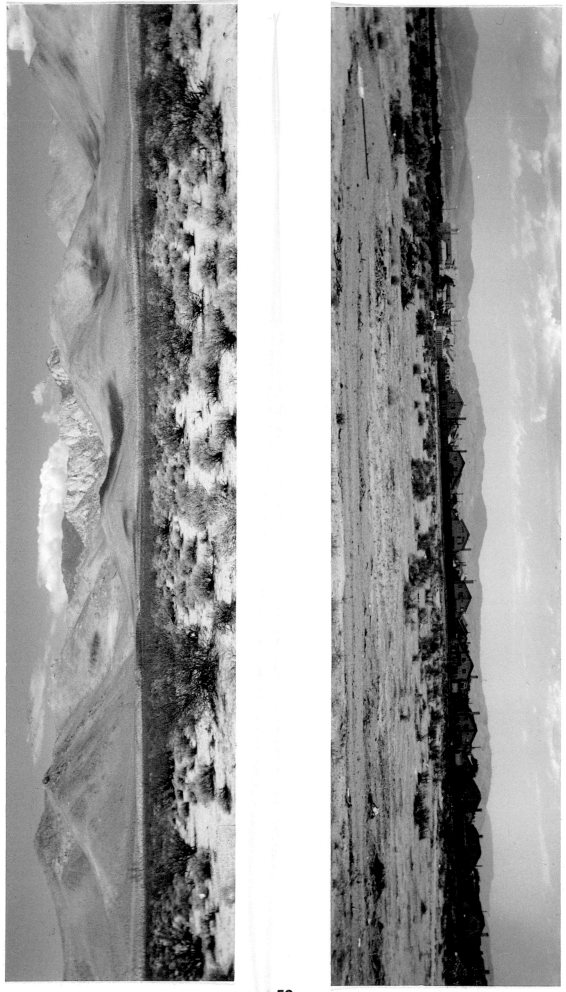

For Californians, the garden ("Home on the Range") and wilderness (*On the Road*) locations of paradise seesaw back and forth as fast as each possibility is projected onto the screen, erased by the next rectangle of flashing lights and by the next.

Myth makers map our autobiographies, and in California facts have always been fiction. Californians were amusing themselves living in theme parks long before Disneyland. "Facade landscapes" fake an aura of history that we crave: there is Venice in Venice, California; Forest Lawn's Eden-neocropolis in Tropico (now Glendale); Hearst's Castle with zebras roaming the mountains and Italianate colonnades above the Big Sur; Victorian decor and clapboard palazzos, Fisherman's Wharfacades and Grant Avenue's Pagodaland in San Francisco; Ruskinesque *News from Nowhere* rustic in Mill Valley; Satan's Las Vegas in God's garden at Tahoe; and International Style beach houses for domestic festivities at the beach. California is high on seductive illusions of throwaway landscapes (and people). Tradition sells better recycled as the latest style.

The Spanish Colonial Revival, perfected and enforced by zoning legislature in Santa Barbara, is the most popular style for paradise. Since Helen Hunt Jackson's successful book *Ramona* (1884) sentimentalized picturesque images of Mission Style red-tiled roofs, whitewashed walls, and lush gardens as our Eden that never was, this myth has become the preferred way for Californians to see themselves. In California, Eden is a big house with fake Mexican decor, and real Mexican gardeners sitting on a plot of English lawn.

Charles Fletcher Lummis (on the payroll of the *Los Angeles Times* and the Chamber of Commerce, a Los Angeles invention) edited the popular *Out West: Land of Sunshine*. One of the first cult magazines (*Sunset, California Living, California Now* and *L.A. Style* were to follow), it "created a comprehensive fiction of Southern California as the promised land of a millenarian Anglo-Saxon racial odyssey. They inserted a Mediterraneanized idyll of New England life into the perfumed ruins of an innocent but inferior 'Spanish' culture. In doing so, they wrote the script for the giant real-estate speculations of the early twentieth century that transformed Los Angeles from small town to metropolis. Their imagery, motifs, values and legends were in turn endlessly reproduced by Hollywood, while continuing to be incorporated into the ersatz landscapes of suburban Southern California" (Mike Davis).

Making myths is now called public relations. In 1910, before droughts, overpopulation, and pollution problems, it was said that "For all alike the country-side is golden, the sun warm, the sky blue, the birds joyous, and the spring young in the land. The climate is positively guaranteed. It will not rain; it will shine, the stars will watch" (Steward Edward White). The propaganda of the time was amazingly erroneous even when true.

The Island of California was seen golden before green became a more fashionable color. As soon as that flaw of nature, and the myth makers, was recognized, it was corrected. Never mind that most of California was an oasis civilization and that Hispanic agrarian methods dealt with the droughts. Rolling English lawns conveyed the right image. If people wanted California to look like Eden, it had to be painted green.

The yellow desert was watered and green gardens grew.

Without water there is no illusion, no suburbs, and no California. Myths, and the politics of hydrology, can move mountains. Water in the West is the one uncontrollable force of nature that can be controlled; it is also the one element of nature that we lack. In the West, which begins at the one hundredth meridian, where the rain stops and the wilderness starts, rain is called Godwater.

In California, God smiles on water projects: water is "the fountain of life"; it erases all our sins and restores health and vitality. Every swimming pool can be seen as a piece of nature, ordered, a mirror of God, reflecting His immortality.

In 1773, the Spanish Franciscans constructed a six-mile tiled aqueduct to move water from the San Diego River to Mission San Diego de Alcala. In 1851, the Mormons founded an irrigation colony in San Bernardino based on water and religion: "Oh, faith rewarded!/Now no idle dream. The long-sought/Caanan before him lies;/he floods the desert with the mountain stream,/and lo! It leaps/transformed to paradise" (A Mormon hymn). The Imperial Valley was hailed as "The Egyptian Delta of America;" the Colorado River was our Nile; and when the Salton Sea flooded (naturally), it was seen as "The Dead Sea of the Western Holy land." Slogans were taken as truth: "Rain follows the plough," "Aridity means fertility," "We cultivate and irrigate, but it is God who exaggerates."

The men who promoted public works that civilized the wilderness into a garden were praised for making the desert bloom. Everything was done on a big scale, and fast. The large Mexican *rancheros* were never divided into small landholdings that independent farmers might have turned into a Promised Land of private Edens. The words *Homestead Act* were another name for fraud. Individual settlers anticipating the georgic life read the fine print and stayed home. Those who came worked for the big corporations. By 1870, 516 land speculators owned 8,685,439 acres of California and another 12,000,000 acres were allocated to the railway.

The water was free, the land was free, and the men who got the water to the land controlled the people and the profits. We all know the story from *Chinatown* (1974) and *The Two Jakes* (1990). In California, success is wealth; poverty has always been a sin. Maybe Eden was never intended for the poor.

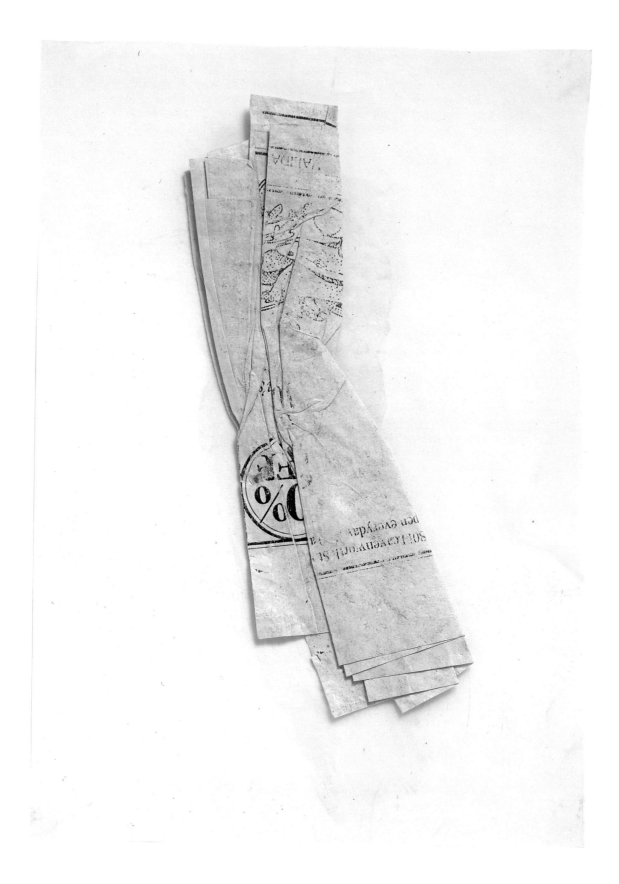

Design for garden.

In California gardens are real estate:
location (a plot, site, tract, or acreage), location (a situation for social mobility), location (scenery for TV, videos, and movies).

Location is everything, and it changes all the time. Location is compensation, spiritual and financial. In the game of upward mobility, things start at the tract. The ideal garden changes with each changing illusion, opportunity, and income bracket. Buyers strive to see themselves in the perfect picture, in "Pasadena Where the Grass Is Greener" (city slogan). "People will buy a backyard, they'll buy friendly neighbors who will smile, they'll buy well-kept lawns" (real estate broker).

To divert the buyer's eyes from bad air and worse traffic, developers provide low-cost, low-maintenance, Lie-A-Lot gardens to hide high prices and cheap construction. To speed sales, myth makers devise ingenious baits and rebates to entice the "ad mass" into grander Edens than they need or can afford.

Plant a freeway on the desert and you grow suburban gardens. California's highways are decorated with gala signs and sequin banners promising free diamond rings, dancing lessons, and Rolls Royces to sweeten real estate deals. "C'mon. There's a beautiful new dream house out there just waiting for your family. With a long list of incentives including landscaping and decor packages. And no-cost closing. To make that dream a reality" (ad in the *Los Angeles Times*).

There is no formal difference between the site plan for a golf course, a Planned-Unit Development and Forest Lawn: playing games, playing house, and playing dead. All take place on, or under, identical green lawns and offer similar familiar amenities. All three are sanctuaries where, supposedly, everything is picturesque, picture perfect, and controlled: nature, the water supply, the neighbors, happiness, and the children. In the better PUDs, rules of decor and decorum, plus tricks of scale taught at design schools, control undesirable, borrowed, and hidden views. Marketable styles, advertising, and infrastructure make the gardens grow. Lawns hide the underground politics and pipes. Berms and bushes conceal hook-ups, plug-ins, pop-ups, timers, utility boxes, and the neighbors.

For the well-fixed and frightened, suburban Edens imply sweet dreams rather than urban nightmares. They see life in the city taking place on noisy, dangerous, straight streets, whereas safety, privacy, and quiet occur along the safe wiggly paths of suburbia. Democratic freedom in the Western wilderness has ended up as self-imposed confinement in the garden. A two-hour commute is the price of fear. Freedom is fear: fear of city streets, dirt, disorder, decay, and the wrong people. Success is a Utopian castle secure behind a carefully greened Arcadia. Zoning law acts "as barbed-wire social fencing." The drought is secretly welcomed by people who use it as a God-given excuse to stop hook-ups for new, low-cost, which means undesirable, housing.

In the new California suburbs, they build the (white) walls first. Behind these (sound?) barriers Homeowner Association Restrictions (HAs, like the hypocritical, "invisible" ha-has of the English gentry) guard the private turf. Gate houses, with invisible electronic eyes and visible security guards, announce and inhibit every entrance. "Gated communities" is the new name for "neighborhoods." The streets inside are wide and empty, ready for a *Gunfight at the OK Corral* (1959). People are scared indoors, behind walls of inoperable picture windows, with the drapes drawn, locked entrances and garage doors, and high fences. The rich boast secret terrorist-proof security rooms hidden in the bowels of their homes.

It is comforting to live in houses and gardens with neighbors of the same class, with the same incomes, the same high-tech toys and pop-consumer gadgets, consuming the same microwaved pink popcorn, golden ads, green aspirations, and technicolor illusions. Once inside, it is easy not to see what is outside. These gardens are ornamental, hypocritical pieces of decorated dirt where people's myths of politics, money, racism, sex, and fashion are played out—if they can afford it.

Gardens for the really rich are sanctuaries inherited or highly leveraged. They are "virtual realities" of extraordinary botanical showmanship for performing private rituals and forbidden games. Garden styles are in good taste: French Formal Mediterranean/Semi-Tropical with *allées* for grand entrances, axes for cocktail party strolling, and broad terraces with long views pretending to own all they survey; or English/New England/Semi-Italinate with Great Lawns, like bankrolls, rolling down toward the Pacific, and silver scrims of hot air rising from the heated pool as a private line to paradise. The best are too exclusive to be photographed; the only fear is of being caught using too much rationed water.

For the upwardly mobile, moving from one leveraged property sale to the next, there are more varied, and vulgar, garden styles: Country Club/Pee-Wee Golf Course/Picturesque with exotics and self-conscious specimens. In Northern California people tend to hide their wealth behind high hedges; in Southern California it is well displayed on the front lawn. A piece of lawn, the bigger the better, demonstrates the owner's control over enough youth, water, and wealth to keep the grasses green.

Gentlemen come from gentle hills; shabby lawns mean shabby people. In Alameda, after five years of drought, the Navy ordered people in military housing to water their lawns, to make everything green and shipshape, or risk eviction. Landlords feel that growing vegetables where there should be a front lawn might indicate that the owner can no longer afford to purchase his produce from the supermarket.

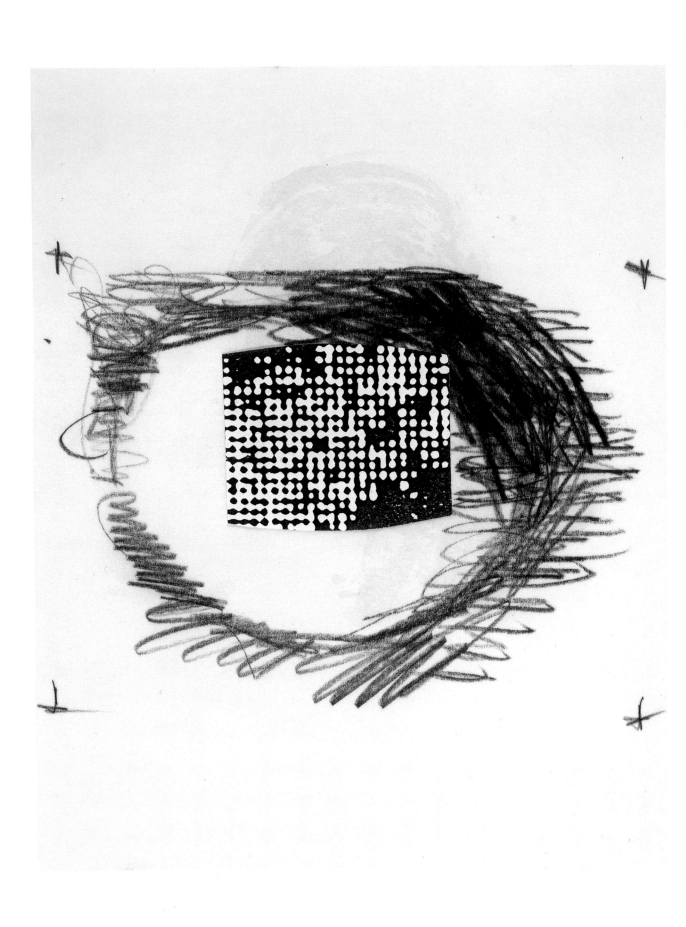

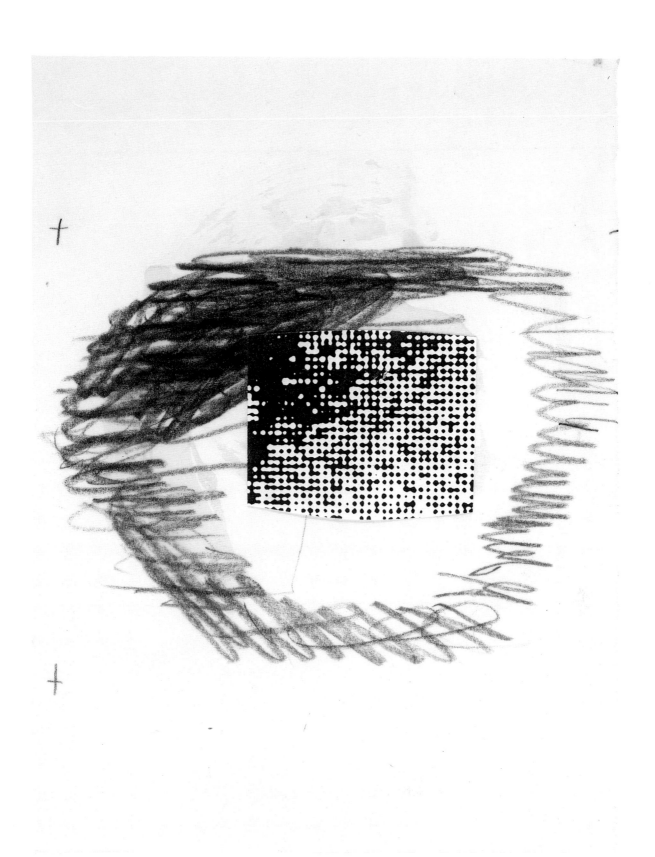

Most suburban gardens are designed to look remarkably similar. The prescription is a winding path, lots of lawn, clumps of scrubbish, "showy color, and "special effects" scattered as if by God, plus whatever is available at the local nursery.

Gardens of the Modern Movement are designed to look natural, or like abstract expressionist paintings. The aim is to make a romantic wilderness in which a white architectural folly looks as if it just happens to appear.

Urban backyards in San Francisco vary from Pacific Heights Formal, where you can imagine picnicking at Versailles, to St. Francis Woods Picturesque, with memories of lunch in Yorkshire. In the Mission and Marina Districts are Mexican pepper and fruit trees, Italian arbors and vegetable gardens. In the Financial District are greenhouses on rooftops growing orchards of orchids.

For the conscientious there are appropriate political garden styles. Conservative Republican capitalists in Southern California delight in golf course-sized lawns with tall palms ejaculating in front of the house. Liberal Democrat capitalists in the north prefer viewing their vineyards vignetted by oaks or redwood groves in the rear. For the politically righteous, the correct style is "Gardening Without Water." The Xeriscape Center is using "dry water," a formula gel in which the bacteria does the watering. "Un-plants," garden decorations made of styrofoam and polyester silk-screened green and gorgeous live forever if they don't melt in the desert sun.

In drought-resistant gardens, what used to be called "weeds" are now admired as "natural grasses," and if you mow them you have a lawn not green, but golden.

When they turn off the water in California we can restyle our gardens to a formerly anticipated Mediterranean allusion. We can return to yellow hills of baeria, gold sun-ups, and orange poppies scattered with black cypresses and oaks, fields of wild cyclamen, herbs, and roses, pink gilias, blue and lavender lupin, nemophilasm, irises, and lilacs; more nobal cacti and heliotropes will release their hot smells over the fields in summer. White villas are already replacing redwood ranch houses; fields of lavender and orchards of olives are preferred to water-guzzling petunias and artificial green lawns.

Voltaire told us to cultivate our garden, but what if water is rationed and the dirt on the ground costs five hundred dollars a square foot?

For the poor there are public parks: Golden Gate, Aquatic, Dolores, and Washington Square in San Francisco; Will Rogers State Beach, Exposition, Echo, and Elysian Parks in L.A., all shared with dope dealers and the homeless. There are supermarket malls, outdoor fast-food plazas, and benches under laurel trees on busy streets. There are fishing piers where you can walk on water straight out onto the Pacific at Half Moon Bay, Santa Cruz, Santa Monica, and Seal Beach. There are campsites from Anza Borreggo to Inyo to Tamalpias and the Klamath for people with trucks and sleeping bags. There is splendor at the Palace of Fine Arts, at Ocean Beach's palm-lined Promenade, and at the traditional green town squares in Sonoma and Brawley. There are picnic benches at the end of bus lines, at Crissy Field and Imperial Beach. Close to home, there are foundation planting and flower pots.

For every Californian there are designer parking lots blooming with extraordinarily colored makes and models; there are gas stations and strip cities decorated with plots of Astroturf, greener than grass and more environmentally responsible.

The gardens most people see most of the time are the freeway embankments; palms heralding off-ramps with the same cool elegance they once displayed at the entrances to private homesteads, landscapes of eucalyptus and pepper trees where appropriate, white sand and sea grasses along the Pacific, pines in the Sierras, and green grass announcing all the suburbs. Every view framed by somebody's windshield is somebody else's garden.

Gardens go by on the highways: truckloads of tied palms, horizontal, desert-hardy trees and shrubs, and rolls of sod lawn, destined to become instant landscapes in Palmdale and Riverside.

California is where people have paved "the future to strike a line of purpose across it for somewhere" (Robert Frost).

Life, liberty, and the pursuit of mobility, California style, is being in your car with freeway CONDITIONS CLEAR, your tank full, and the music on loud. Then you feel you're going someplace. Your car is your skin, your costume, and your privacy. You are in control. In your car, or truck, or RV, all California is your garden, without walls. Each individual can move forward in his high-tech bubble to turn on, and turn off, at whichever green rectangle seems, at the moment, to offer the most desirable Eden.

The green rectangle of paradise is now the glossy, green highway sign promising freedom on the FREE-ways, announcing the next possibility, and the next. You just have to choose.

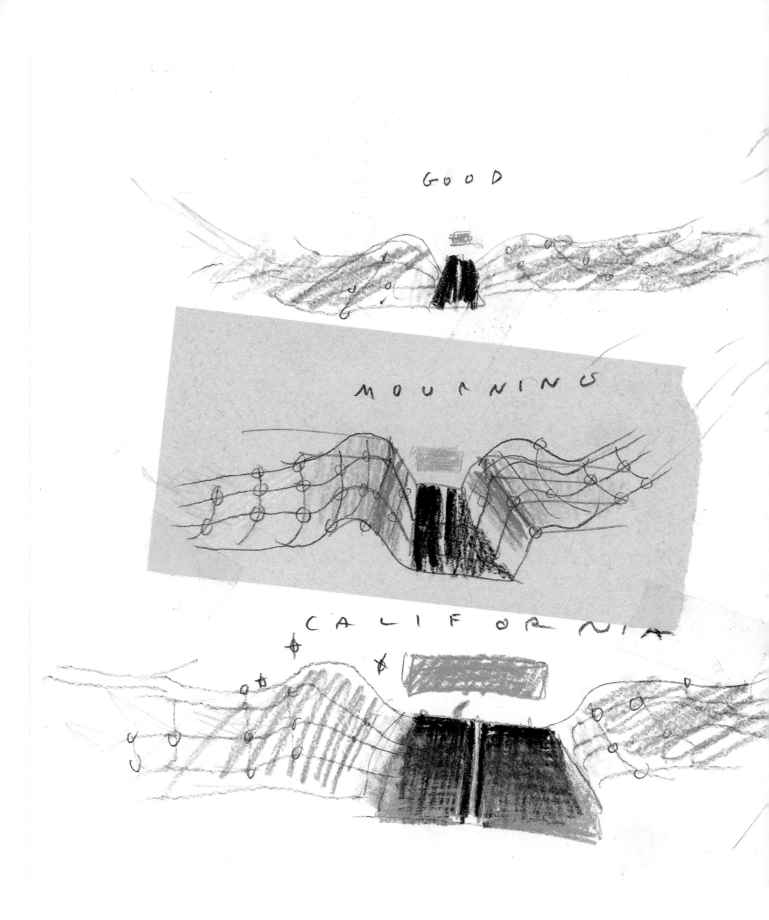

the Green Rectangle of Paradise

# LANDSCAPES

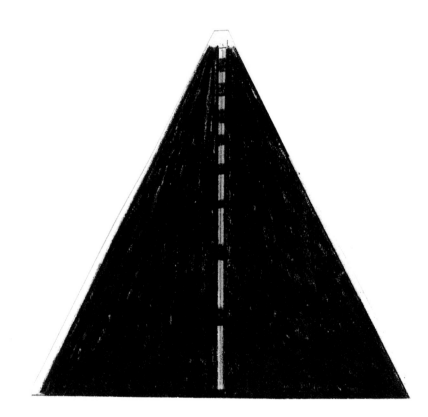

the Night Oakland was Burning.

In California, landscapes are everything we see, and don't see, following the yellow line to vanishing points out of sight.

When the Franciscan friars scattered mustard seeds along the roads from Mission to Mission, they made the first yellow lines, of mustard blossoms, for travelers to follow. Paint yellow lines or dashes down the middle of a strip of black asphalt and the ritual begins. Everyone follows them everywhere.

Landscapes in California are what you see in the distance. They are views on the horizon that no one person owns, but everyone possesses. They are the groundwork, backgrounds, views, fragments, and leftovers that you can't destroy; you just change what you look at.

Californians think with our eyes. We focus, for an instant, on a point of view, a target, a sight, or a site, inside the frame; but most of the time we look at the landscape with an aware inattention to the vast, and the vague. Landscapes include the fuzzy out-of-focus stuff outside the frame that changes with each movement of the eye or aperture, the mood or the wind.

Landscapes are what we ignore, or forget, since we didn't stop to take a picture. They are any view you happen to catch in a grab shot, or from a camera mounted on a car frame, clicking off images at programmed, or random, intervals while speeding over the State.

**Splendid landscapes, and spectacular faults, slash up and down California:**

To the west, the coastline is 1,264 miles of blaze, ten yards wide, and the center of the universe for Californians who feel they must live within sight of the Pacific.

To the east, deserts and high mountains separate California from the continent. The Sierra Nevada, the Klamath, Santa Lucia, Transverse, Panamint, and Peninsular ranges stand north and south.

Up and down the middle are fault lines, visible and hidden; the San Andreas, Hayward and Calaveras, the Owen Valley and San Jacinto, make the mountains and the cities and the people constantly quake. In just a few million years, the San Andreas fault will move Los Angeles north, side by side with San Francisco.

The main waterways go north and south. The natural rivers, the Sacramento and the San Joaquin, the Klamath, Eel, Russian, and Salinas rivers; the Delta, the San Francisco Bay, Lake Tahoe, the Salton Sea, and the Colorado River borderline, are drawn vertically on the map. The 444-mile California Aqueduct, bringing water from the Northern rivers to the Southern deserts, is the longest artificial water garden in the world.

Eight-lane highways, or eight-foot dirt roads, go almost everywhere. You can get up before dawn to drive west to the beach or east into the sunrise, but the longest lifelines go up and down the state. There is Highway 1 from Capistrano Beach to Leggett, and the Pacific Coast Highway along the beaches, with cliffs fast eroding into beaches. Highway 1 connects, when it is forced away from the Pacific, to Highway 101, the old El Camino Real, until, north of Eureka, 101 hits the Pacific and heads north to Crescent City. Or, you can start from Calexico up 222 or 86, around the Salton Sea, to 10 and 215, and then take the astonishing 395. 395 goes through the Mohave and along the Eastern Sierra, past Mt. Whitney, 14,887 feet straight up to the west, and the desert to Death Valley straight out to the east. Highway 99 connects the old Central Valley towns, but you have to get back on 395 to get all the way north to the Shasta-Cascade, still called "wilderness."

Route I-5 goes straight, and fast, from Tijuana to Oregon. The road reaches up to you and everything is at a distance. There are no stop signs on I-5. The yellow lines of paint point relentlessly ahead. With an RV-castle-on-wheels you never need to leave the road. Glossy green rectangles in the sky announce place names out of sight that you can vaguely notice, and ignore. There are GAS/FOOD/LODGING minimarket pit stops and Scenic Rest Areas for a quick memory fix with the click of a camera. When someone invents solar-powered mobile homes, every Californian will get one as their birthright to pursue perpetual happiness in motion up and down California.

In California there are drive-in restaurants, movies, churches, supermarkets, banks, insurance claim offices, and parties, and drive-by art and shootings. Politicians are talking about using the freeway system's "straight, simple, and neutral . . . natural community borders" to redefine electoral districts. With a full tank you're an adventurer in AutomobileLand twenty-four hours a day; when the tank is empty you're homeless.

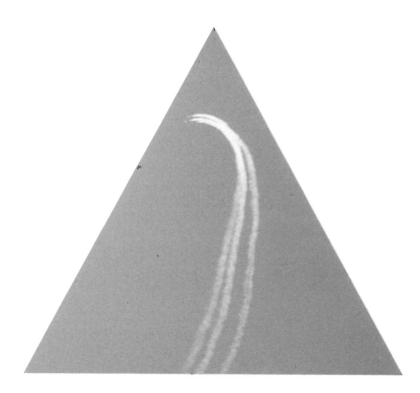

Formerly, it was said that California was divided across the middle into Northern California, focused on San Francisco and the past, and Southern California, looking toward Los Angeles and the future. New census data, vote tallies, economic lineups, political directions, chains of electronic blips, flight paths, hidden infrastructures, visible power lines, invisible lines of communication, and ways of life, connect everything up and down the State.

Sensational stripes, strips, and strip cities zap north and south:

The Pacific Metroplex/crystal-gazing "Fortunate Coast"/Reynar Banham's "Surfurbia" begins as the Gold Coast at Orange County and extends north to *Vineland* (Thomas Pynchon) and the Jedi's foggy redwood forests. There are people, mostly natives, who feel that if you aren't in sight of the Pacific you're living in the Midwest; in Port Hueneme they have imposed a "view tax" on unencumbered views of the Pacific. The Coast's megaloparadise contains the most expensive homes and the most homeless; the best scenery and the worst pollution; High Art and low employment; and two-thirds of the population. There is a strong "nimby" ("not in my back yard," or better, "not on my lawn") compulsion to use environmental issues and controls to stop everything and everybody.

The Inland Empire begins at the Imperial and extends up through the Conchella Valley, Riverside, and San Bernardino counties to the Central Valley. It is four hundred miles long, fifty miles wide, and booming. Three-fifths of California's seventeen-billion-dollar per year agribusiness is here. Inland, everything is GO for more green fields watered into green bucks. A moratorium on new water hook-ups is another word for death. The big sign over the Irrigation Store in Morena Valley (the fastest growing bedroom community in the state) reads RAIN FOR SALE. New residents in the Inland Empire are people who can't afford to live on the coast, or those who have tried it and fled to a seemingly more safe, sane, and unpolluted paradise.

Both the Glittering Coast and the Inland Empire are now outgrowths of Los Angeles. L.A. is not just a city: it is a fast-selling commodity that sold itself up and out over California and the rest of the world. L.A., a greenhouse growing the eccentricities of the twentieth century, is being promoted as the "world city" of the twenty-first. Even critics ridiculing this "L.A. 2000 Jewel of the Pacific Rim" propaganda are misread as hype.

L.A. invented its landscape myths, made and moved into them, and proceeded to transmit them everywhere. Everything happens "new and hot" in L.A. first, and faster.

L.A. BRINGS IT ALL TOGETHER is the slogan of the *L.A. Times*; THE CITY CAME INTO BEING TO PRESERVE LIFE, IT EXISTS FOR THE GOOD LIFE is the slogan wrapped around the City Hall and the citizens.

Free spirits, and aging Midwesterners, want to find paradise without problems or limitations. Los Angeles promises a garden party, and everybody comes. Movie myths show images of L.A. leading to happy endings, and even physical planners are not immune. Free urban sprawl is equated with political freedom. In L.A. some planners, usually from out of town, plan; others see unplanned pastoralism as an art form and fear that any rules imposed on "the self-regulating chaos" would destroy the look of this wilderness that they love. The fun is in breaking the rules.

L.A. is a dreamland "reproducing itself endlessly across the desert with the assistance of pilfered water, cheap immigrant labor, Asian capital, and desperate home buyers willing to trade lifetimes on the freeway in exchange for $500,000 'dream homes' in the middle of Death Valley" (Mike Davis).

L.A. is a landscape "conceived largely as a series of real-estate promotions but supported largely by a series of confidence games, a community currently afloat on motion pictures and junk bonds and the B-2 Stealth bomber, the conviction that something can be made of nothing" (Joan Didion).

Originally a health resort promoted to cure consumption, L.A. grew into the capital of consumption; L.A. is the capital of capital; the rules of the power play are written by capitalism. Nature is real estate, gardens grow greenbacks, and landscapes are golden opportunities. When you look at a mountain you think escrow. "A lot in Beverly Hills alters your Being" (L.A. realtor).

Despite accurate ominous observations, L.A. boosters still boast: they counter that it is precisely the "dramatic growth" that makes it possible for manufacturing to thrive; they say that water problems are "improving dramatically," we have merely to cover more agricultural land with developments and then use the 85 percent agri-land water allotment for growing suburbs; they point to the fact that in 1991 40 percent more businesses moved to L.A. than ran away and that California has the largest GNP in the world. Fourteen-and-a-half million people live in the L.A./Anaheim/Riverside empire, and they can still boast more private Places in the Sun than any other paradise on earth.

L.A. is a city without frames, unless you say (and only a nervous visitor would) that the freeways frame and fragment the gridded ground below. For Angelinos, the serpentine freeways flying through the sky are rivers rushing over the city making everything everywhere accessible.

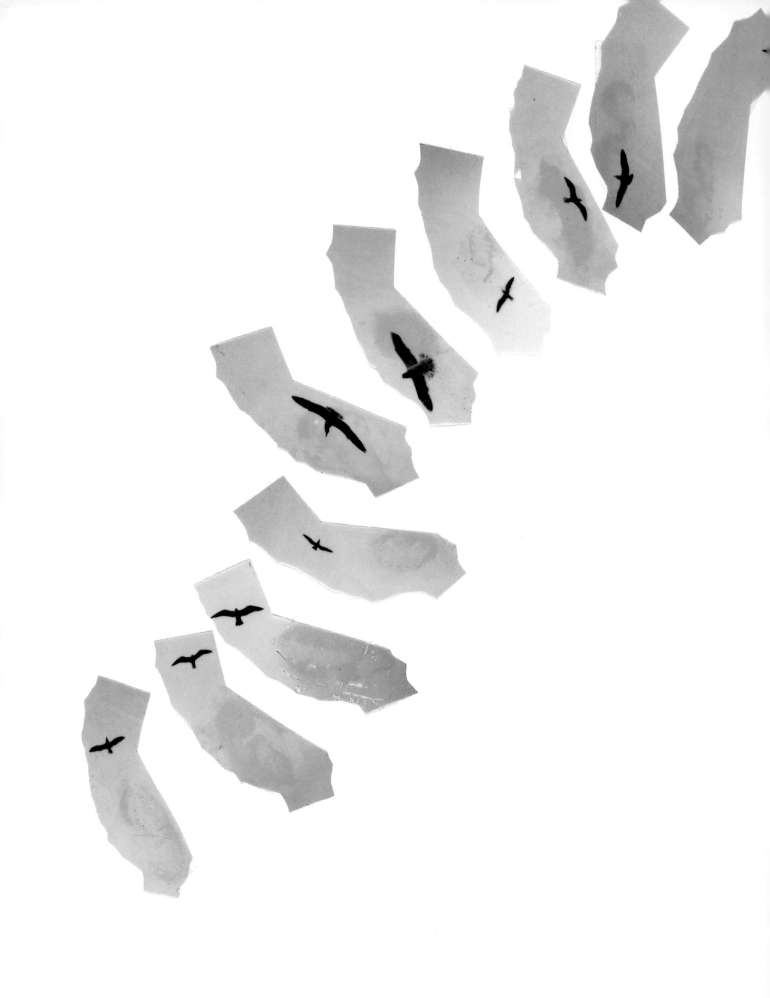

Without freeways, there are no myth, no movement, and no California landscapes:

On the freeway, "The life force is under the hood of the automobile" (Timothy Tyler). In *L.A. Story* (1990) God is a lovable electronic freeway sign that knows all, wants to be hugged, talks in riddles, and gives the hero advice for the lovelorn in flashing blips of light.

From the freeway California is a collection of supermarket/treasure islands, beaches and ski slopes, theme parks and pit stops, connected to locked rooms where you leave your job, your clean shirts, and your children.

From the freeway you are at the right height to see every possibility on the horizon from a distance; you look up and out, not down. There are signs naming towns you seem to know without ever having to bother to visit them; you go in directions you never meant to go in order to get to where you think you want to be. If there is nowhere to go, just keep going.

Suspended monetarily by a few inches of hot air in lifesavers made of black rubber, we rush from one view of the landscape to the next. The images we see are different and the same. **Which view of the landscape is California?**

For people on the move, California is an optical effect where figures on the screen appear to rush toward the observer with an enormous increase in size, only to dwindle away even faster into the distance. The changing views are fuzzy, unfixed, and transfixing. Unframed. We anticipate them, see them big, and never see them again.

For most of us, landscapes are what we see from the freeway. They are what we move over, around, and into. We are where they are. We rush through landscapes and the landscapes swallow us up.

California offers a lot of land to move through and maneuver on. The land is young; you can hear the contours creep. The people are young; they rush around, incessantly, changing landscapes and lifestyles. Californians are a race of people racing. There is a buzz on the surface of things.

Driving on California's freeways, each acid-colored sight seems unforgettable until, over the next rise, it is forgotten. The transfixed hours spent rushing to space out on space are the only peace and privacy most people ever know. With the "rapture-of-the-freeway. The mind goes clean. The rhythm takes over" (Joan Didion). We are free to pray to any god and let our spirit rise coolly upward. The game is getting our bodies past the next potential crash with steel.

In California a driver's license is our Identity Card. We use it as license to move through the landscape as if we own it. We speed around looking for the images that movies and lyrics tell us are out there. Our cars are the machines that get us to the gardens of California. No longer is there "no there there" because "there" is everywhere we go.

Take the wheel and you take the world. "We're children of the freeway with speedin' in our veins" (Mega Death). *On the Road*, with no helmet (a fighting word) on your head, all your senses are in high gear. "My 1979 Harley FXE is my home in the country, my freedom in the fresh air, my last frontier" (helmet protestor).

"The road's what counts. Just look at the road. Don't worry about where it's goin'" (a Sam Shepard character).

Cars have been infused with mythological powers of freedom, strength, sex, status, and happiness by the ads that sold them, and us.

In your new Jaguar XJ-S convertible you have "A Place In The Sun That Moves Like The Wind" (1990 advertisement).

Driving on Sunset Boulevard in a Jaguar is a spiritual experience: the top's down and the water parts, people look at you differently; you feel different, you feel like an "If you only have one life to live, live it as a blond" blond.

Fast cars, fast food, fast women, and free spirits are on the road. Natives and tourists, the displaced and misplaced, drive hard to live "life in the fast lane."

The game is more pace than place. If Californians change lanes and channels fast enough; they transcend to whatever they want to be.

**Is California?          2.  A performance piece?**

As people move around the landscape,
they move the landscape around.

Men and women come to California to
possess the geography in order to
change it; once here, they make new
horizons, new skylines, new lives, and
new money. Landscapes are made by
private fantasies and public ventures;
they are manipulated by exploiting egos
and manufactured by quiet residents.
Each person who plants a tree or cuts
one down, each housewife or hydrologist,
traffic engineer or merchant, promoter,
politician, or street sweeper plays the
game of juggling scale and color, objects
and images that adds to the accidents
our fathers made which we live in.

Landscapes are made and erased as fast
as they are dreamed up. Each California
landscape is changed to make the next
one.

Landscapes are idiosyncratic and
intense, flamboyant and skillful,
accidental, empty, vague, and
impressive; they are beautiful, ugly,
rough, and terrible; continuously
changing rearrangements of everything
we make, move around, and move
through. Everybody's Public Art.

In California the landscape is our
Museum of Natural/Unnatural History,
and the exhibitions are changing all the
time. Mountain cropping is site specific.
Planting trees is a performance piece.
Carving highway cuts through mountains
is monumental sculpture. Driving through
the landscapes, traffic signs and billboard
art are all some people see. "Finish
fetish" objects project our illusions. A
shiny new car parked in the driveway is
each owner's private art exhibition. The
worst hell-as-heaven realities, crack on
the streets and cracks in the
superstructures, deconstruct into the
latest MTV performances and high art.
Our daily fix of catharsis is viewed, fast
and almost free, on the nightly TV news.
Even the sunsets are more spectacular
through the smog.

California is an island,
an illusion, and a whore:
'she' always was.

For gold-leafed ladies and determined gentlemen, California is where paradise, progress, and expectation still seem possible. In California myths teach us how to live, and since no one can remember the past, the future always looks golden.

Karl Marx asked a friend to send him some "meaty" reports of California "because nowhere else has the upheaval most shamelessly caused by capitalist centralization taken place with such speed."

Somewhere out here is where dreams come true. This land of the free is the home of the children and grandchildren of sod-busters who, when they plowed *The Virgin Land* into the Dust Bowl (actually, it was because of the success of tractor salesmen, not the failure of nature, that "Dust Follows The Plow"), desperately needed a dream, hit the road, and headed out to Oz. Movies make heroes of gypsies, not peasants. From 1935 to 1939 six thousand people a month came to California. Now sixty thousand a month come to live here.

Growth is essential for the continued success of our five-hundred-billion-dollar economy. The 1990 census reports that the 30,888 million people, the fifty-two member House delegation, and the fifty-four electoral votes—one-fifth of those needed to elect a president—give California more clout than any state has had since the beginning of the Republic. We will probably have double the population of New York in ten years. If we were a nation we would be the seventh most powerful on earth. As things are going, by 2010 the population of California will be fifty million (Leon Bouvier).

California is a landscape of economic and photo opportunities. There has been one land boom after another: gold, agriculture, oil, tourism, and real estate. We have a boomtown mentality.

Whether true or false, the story has it that Elbert P. Jones, a doctor and the editor of the *California Star*, owned more nuggets and gold dust than any man in California. Gold was his passion. The doctor spread sheets on his bedroom floor, then sheets of gold on his sheets; he would then wiggle his naked toes in the gold dust, shower handfuls over his head and shoulders, and roll in the glittering substance.

In our Cali-pop-cycle of pleasures, there is a Dreamland Fantasy Tour in Palm Springs where, for seven thousand dollars, you can walk on streets that stars might have walked on once. Beverly Hills High struck oil in their playground to help pay for higher education; and in Marina De Rey, "The sand seemed cleaner than other sand and the water seemed bluer and the breezes seemed kinder . . . for the Chosen in the land of the free . . . who seemed to have escaped the daily grind of living"(Charles Bukowski, *Hollywood*).

For fast-footed hedonists who feel that "Sun is Fun" and "Sin is In," California is the perfect playground. Despite statistics of despair, tourists arrive. They rent an apartment, and after three weeks call themselves Californians. They change their style of car, mate, diet, and muscle definition. The local propaganda, subterfuge, fast cuts, smooth fades, narcissism, and amnesia convince them that the barrage of fool's gold was, might have been, and might be paradise. The word is "Go West": California is the political Disneyland/Superbowl Game of 1992; everybody wants a ticket to the second Gold Rush. Even the space shuttle comes home to California.

Aldous Huxley, who lived in Los Angeles, understood that "Those who have been to Paradise agree that there is a lot of glittering gold material there." Paradise as plethora, where all your needs are fulfilled, was fast followed by paradise as luxury, where everything beyond need is needed. Free enterprise, private property, luck, ingenuity; the highest mountain, the lowest desert, the biggest ocean; myths and movies make this precarious piece of geography, planned by God and Disney, "the best of all possible worlds."

California is Mother Earth who never dies; "she" just freshens up her makeup.

For up-and-coming newcomers, California is Mother Nature with a facelift: "she" looks great. But facelifts are expensive, temporary, and they make everything look alike.

The unique has become uniform. All that was local is global; everything global is displayed in the local theme parks. L.A.'s concrete roller coaster used to be unusual, now it's a Vogue Pattern for the future; Sunset Strip's neon walls of glitz were vulgar, now every city has them; Marin County's hot-tubs-in-the-wilderness decor was unconventional, now it's big business; Berkeley was infamous for riots, now it's famous for the finest California cuisine. Everything exotic is franchised at Tacobell, Thai Takeout, Pizza Delight, and the Sushi Express. The Matterhorn is in Anaheim and the jungle's in Africa, USA.

Advertising, singing out into us from all the media, mirrors the world brighter than the original, and everybody gleefully buys into its wonderland. Who can resist seeing themselves retouched, glamorous, lounging around the pool in a Pacific garden? That "pushy latecomer, the first world pushed for increased monotony" (Paul Feyerabend), and we all succumbed to its comfort and ambivalence.

Technology, a game where being deceived is taken for granted, is a natural for California.

Technological advertising speeds up everything and lets Big Brother get to you faster.

Technological propaganda is imperceptible, pervasive, and Telerobots seem to have more fun. Movie landscapes are totally computer-generated in Lucas Valley by Industrial Light and Magic. Santa Clara Valley was fifty miles of orchard; now it's fifty miles of Silicon Valley. Aren't industrial parks and supermarkets less monotonous than grids of trees, though orchards can be painted into prettier pictures?

At the University of California at Davis, biotechnologist Clarence I. Kado is working on nature that lights up the world: there are oleanders to illuminate freeway medians, blue shrubs to outline airport runways, and Christmas trees that will glow in the dark. On the Berkeley campus, Lofti Zadeh developed a branch of computer science known as "fuzzy logic", which has been applied to help make our landscapes less imperfect. Fuzzy cameras ensure sharp images, fuzzy TVs automatically brighten as the room darkens, and fuzzy air-conditioners automatically keep the climate ideal.

Private gardens, supposedly a last chance for individual expression, are now predictable. You can buy a disc and enter the dimensions, soil content, and topography of your yard into the computer; press the right buttons, and "with breathtaking speed" your "smart machine" produces full-color plans, elevations, sections, and perspectives. In this *Brave New World* of computers, everybody's paradise can be a garden of acceptable delights. You only have to grow the plants to look like the printouts; perfect and perfectly monotonous.

Anonymity is the latest fad: noism is the new religion. There is Alcoholics Anonymous, Sexaholics Anonymous, Molesters Anonymous, and Overachievers Anonymous. Originality is out; freedom is being free to conform. Catalogues advertise "uni-clothing" that can, and should, be worn by anybody, anywhere. The most fashionable landscapes are those where "there is no there there." You can stop any building project, but it's almost impossible to start or complete something. Politicians and developers who want to get anything done talk about what they are not for. . . .

Weightless points of light prop up our unbearable efforts to outrun all the latest trends and imperatives. Look young, think thin, act successful, and be seen at all the acceptable places. The proliferation of blond old ladies with tight cheeks and frantic eyes reinforces the suspicion that facelifts are a form of mourning.

"I was unhappy, but I was too happy to realize it" (Steve Martin, *L.A. Story*).

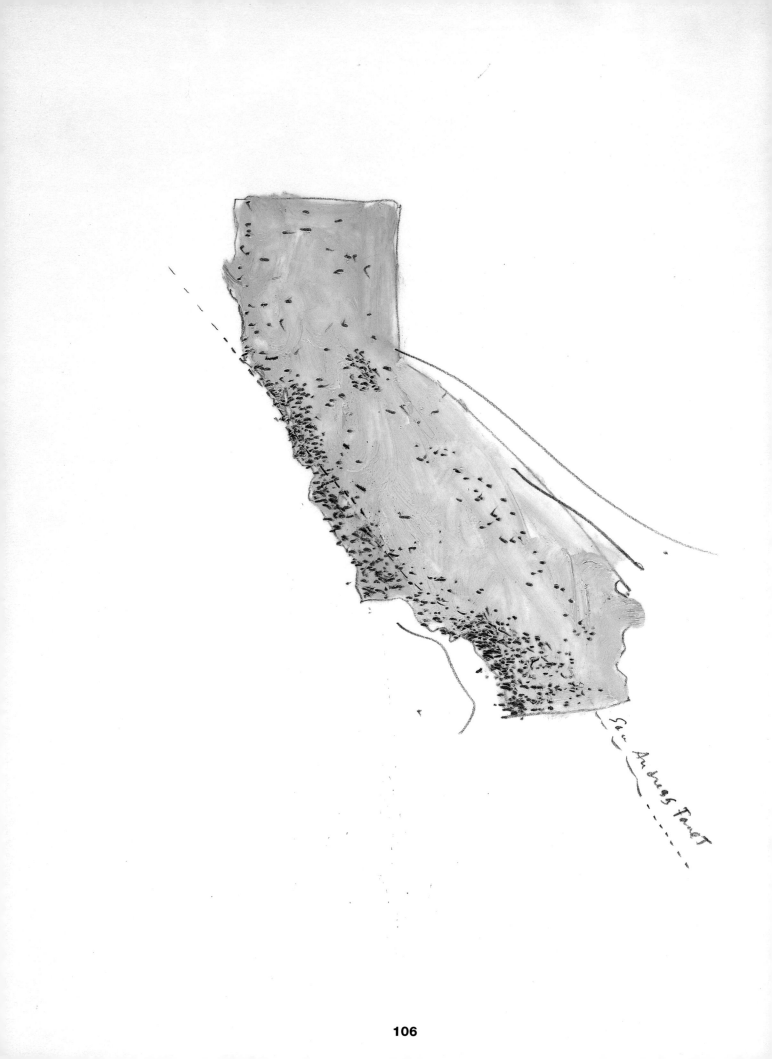

San Andreas Fault

**Is California?   5.   A. Supernova?**

For people caught between razzle-dazzle and resignation, California is supernova: a rarely observed outburst where the maximum intrinsic luminosity increases its light output tremendously and then fades away. Have we loved our landscapes to death? Or has this outburst just been the first two hundred years of nursery school?

Moving to California is everyone's second chance for childhood; living here is acting out perpetual adolescence. We played the game of changing the remote and desolate desert into a prized collection of picture postcards to trade with the other kids, and so far, we've won.

California is Narcissus gazing at the beloved self-image reflected in movie landscapes, TV locations, glossy ad campaigns. We have decorated our contours with tattoos and these landscapes, like advertising, are tattooing the twenty-first century.

California is solipsism: a state in which we assume that we are the only entity that exists. Traveling back to Europe or Asia only seems like going to more Hollywood movies. Someone asked a Californian, "What is your religion?" and he answered, "I think it is California."

For people hypnotized by scanning TV, movie screens, and freeways, California is where each person is the star in his own movie. Everyone writes their own myths and chooses their own changing ways. Driving through the landscape you are part of it. With your face reflected in the car window you are on center screen. The mountains are co-stars. Each mountain provides its own performance, and the happiest mountains are those around the drive-in movie theaters that can see themselves on the big screen.

this is a mirro

**Is California? 6. A virtual reality?**

For people who "want to play mountain ranges on the saxophone" (Jaron Lanier), California is where you can point your hooked-up head upward and fly away into virtual reality.

"What thoughts I have of you tonight, Walt Whitman". Full-bodied in your Datasuit and magic gloves "playing" boundless new colonies, whole worlds within the programmed possibilities of the computer banks. "Unthinkable complexity. Lines of light ranged in the nonspace of the mind, clusters and constellations of data. Like city lights, receding" (William Gibson). No gravity, all gadgets; remapping the landscape of possibilities in a virtual reality that makes novelty more so.

Romantics, visionaries, and corporate technology junkies sit in Silicon Valley "jacking in" and out of landscapes which are everybody's agreed-upon hallucinations. While you are hooked up, everything is beautiful, sexy, and safe. "Harmless as a dream?" You can sit in splendid isolation while you dance with a starlet who takes on the form of a 3-D banana split two miles long, who smells like rain, sounds like the Beach Boys and changes constantly. All that is required is the latest expensive equipment, a visual tolerance for computer graphics, and a high suggestibility. And you are not even polluting the environment.

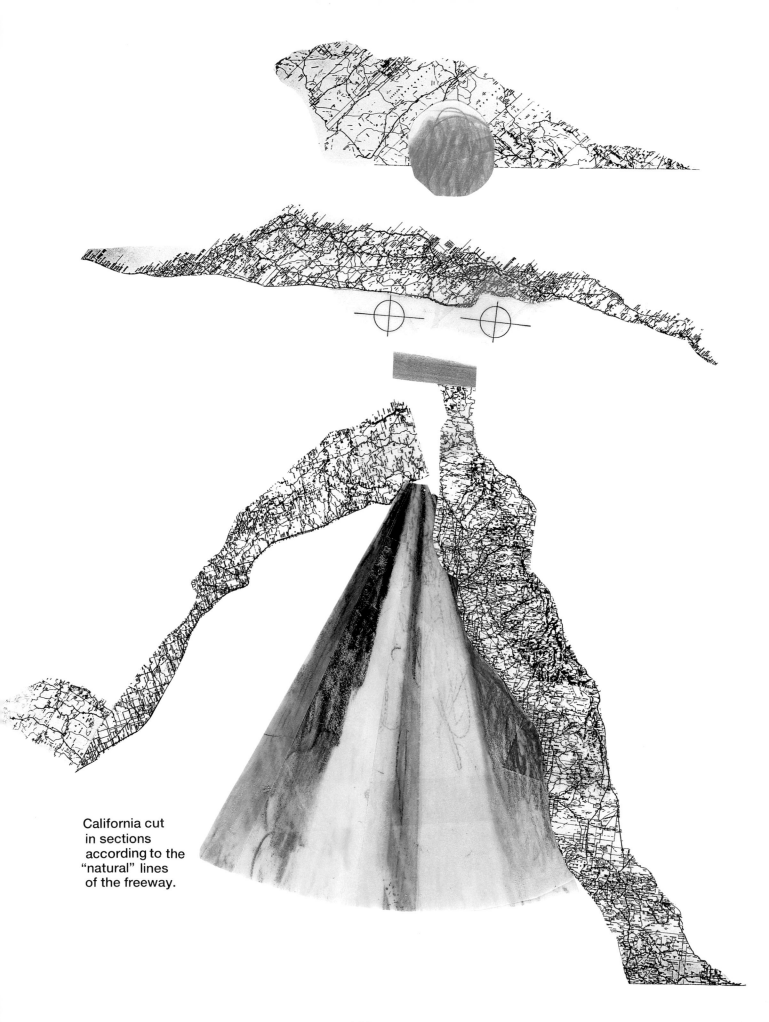

California cut
in sections
according to the
"natural" lines
of the freeway.

For environmentalists, California is a natural wilderness fouled by too much growth, glitz, and greed. When the greenhouse effect melts the polar icecaps, environmentalists see California washed away; opportunists see a Great Glass Greenhouse Mall selling psychedelic scuba gear and houseboats.

In the 1930s, "air and sunshine, because of their deplorable lack of value in exchange, had no reality at all" (Lewis Mumford). In the 1990s clean air and sunshine are our most valued commodities. The landscape is now considered to be more important than the people: if not, there won't be any more people. The questions are: Do oceans and forests have rights? Do trees have legal standing? Do people have ethical obligations to rocks?

For some people it's "You don't know what you've got 'til it's gone. They paved paradise and put in a parking lot" (Joni Mitchell). For others it's our Judeo-Christian God who said to Noah, "I give you everything." He took it. We took it. We used it. After all, "We did not fight and win the wars of the twentieth century to make the world safe for green vegetables" (Richard Darman).

In California there is warfare between groups who want to stop the loggers and those who want to cut down trees. There is a water war among environment, agricultural, and urban interests: among people who want to see water running in rivers, aqueducts, or underground pipes. It is hard to separate romantic nostalgia, apocalyptic wishful thinking, Eco-Fascism, white racism, and fact.

The rules are made by mostly white, upper-middle-class Liberal Conservationists (conservative and radical). NO has replaced GO. The new hero abstains. No more chemical, cigarette, traffic, plastic, fast-food, or sex pollution. No more people; the earth can no longer support them and their emissions. Eco-extremists want to damn Columbus for precipitating the rape of paradise.

When it comes to the "tilling and keeping" of our Garden of Eden as enlightened self-interest, the question is: Which Garden of Eden—the open wilderness or the walled sanctuary? In this last decade of the twentieth century there are two revolutions going on that will probably change the landscapes of the twenty-first century: the Green Revolution and the Greenback Revolution. Each wants to make the landscapes of the twenty-first century into a Garden of Eden, but each envisions a different garden.

With the Green Revolution, the Garden of Eden will be nature as wilderness, preserved, restored, and again environmentally sound. In this natural garden, the spiritual contemplation of nature, a personal and romantic form of transcendental earth worship, will merge with the practical protection of nature, a matter of enlightened survival.

With the Greenback Revolution, the Garden of Eden will be nature recycled as scenic backdrops for walled suburbs and other marketable commodities built and cultivated for a waiting and anxious public. If the landscapes look like Disneyland-treasure island-shopping malls or planned theme-park-suburbs, that will be what was left over from the twentieth century. In this man-made paradise, the economic exploitation of nature will merge with the personal expectation to buy VCRs, green vegetables, and rectangles of lawn, also a matter of survival.

Whether the Green Revolution or the Greenback Revolution, the good guys or the bad guys, everybody's favorite color is green. There is "green hype" and "greentailing" and "green masks," under which different Green Politics and Green Economic interests can hide. Each side uses green words and leaf-like logos: politicans who want to win defer to green issues, manufacturers use green packaging. There are "green products" for "green consumers," green Seals of Approval, and green labels on cosmetics and detergents. Most people really care only that fifteen feet of green forest is saved along the highway so that they will not see the tree-stumped war zones and can shoot photos of the kids next to a redwood.

For poets and heretics, gold diggers, screenwriters in the thirties, refugees, exiles, migrants, transients, the homeless and some trusting natives, California is where people and their myths disappear into the "sun-down sea . . . like a lost and bloody cause."

When Montalvo predicted that "where the danger came, there the safety came also," he anticipated the blithe insouciance that allows Calafía's progeny to hide, enthusiastically and successfully, in their glittering self-delusions.

California is an island on shaky ground. Indian legend has it that after "the Big One," California will again be an island. But no one really believes in the liquefaction of paradise.

In 1877, Clarence King found the "geology itself a matter of the imagination . . . frighteningly free." Muir thrilled to the "noble earthquakes," Mother Nature's orgasms, our ultimate courtship with violence, our channel of creation, and every Californian teenagers rite-of-passage. At Universal Studios the most popular entertainment is the fake earthquake simulation.After the 7.1 quake in 1989,"we were united as friends" (especially a few days later as we watched CNN's images of our earthquake, followed by those of the Berlin Wall seemingly collapsing in its wake).

Living in California is a way of committing suicide without dying. In California we flee death by risking it. The game we play best is speeding down the freeway flirting with disaster. In *Rebel without a Cause* (1955), Jimmy Dean is initiated into manhood by playing chicken; George Lucas's *American Graffiti* (1973, shot in Modesto, where the triumphant arch over the highway reads WATER-WEALTH/CONTENTMENT-HEALTH) is a road movie about drag racing on the way to nowhere. Alfred Hitchcock went on location to benign Bodega Bay, and *The Birds* (1963) began to murder the people. "California is a tragic land—like Palestine, like every promised land" (Christopher Isherwood).

In California, we never used to admit to death. Our media technology advertised perpetual regeneration and kept death hidden under the green grass. Since the green Edens of California are themselves dying, new Hollywood movies feature salvation and reincarnation in other heavenly gardens. Dying in California is now just the next move towards upward mobility, over supernatural freeways to more promising divine locations in space. The landscape for *Defending Your Life* (1990) is a trajectory into the unknown. In *Bill & Ted's Bogus Journey* (1991) the trip into suburban heaven consists of dying, going to hell, and being resurrected as a rock band. The most romantic new hero is a *Ghost* (1990); and many Californians are dreaming of returning to a *Field of Dreams* (1989) in green and blissful Ohio.

To go West is to go into the sunset, to abscond, disappear, and die. Some rational people see the media images from California and never leave their own backyards; some come for a visit, and return home with a vengeance; others rush to the red ball of fire and are burned up.

California as Eve

For people drugged by spectacular short cuts, it is hard to find the main road. California is Eden; fantasized, made fantastic, and fucked up.

The real dirt on California is that it is the future, and it doesn't work. We cut down the mountains and they won't grow back; the Pacific is polluted, freedom is a traffic jam, and the people are poisoning the air which, in turn, is poisoning the people. The deserts are used for war games, Hollywood recycles fairy tales, Mickey Mouse is a rat, and the VCR keeps playing the same old movies. On I-5 Thanksgiving weekend 1991, wind, dust clouds, and speed came together near Coalinga to cause the worst pileup in California history. In Malibu they can't see the sea for the shit and the garbage. We looked at the sun and went blind.

California is a successful $700 billion economic venture dependent on something as unpredictable as the weather. It is a desert temporarily greened by an impermanent source of water. We have mini-mansions decorated with gold water faucets and no water. Agricultural workers, who supply the world with food, don't have enough to eat. In the Monticetto hills, south of Santa Barbara, the rich drill wells to water their lawns; on the flats below, jobs for farmworkers, laborers, and construction workers are drying up.

After the golden dreams and godless consumerism, the fast-track careers and freeways, the new Californian direction is downward mobility. Green lawns are turning into yellow yards; weeds are growing on the freeways. The "Superbug" whitefly (AIDS of agriculture) travels with the wind, spots green fields, and descends to devour them. You leave your mark on the land by just getting through it. Since the land rush of 1984, droughts, toxic pollution, soil erosion, recessions, ethical scandals, the possibilities of litigation, and the problems of maintenance have been our landscape architects.

A 1990 poll in the Bay Area found that people no longer go to San Francisco: the parks are inhabited by the homeless, the plazas stink of urine, and there is rape in the gardens. "I Left My Heart in San Francisco" slashed in a crack on the street.

A 1989 poll in Los Angeles records that about half of the residents would like to move out, and assumes that the other half did not hear the question.

Los Angeles is "a pretty girl with the clap" (Larry Gelbart). On a clear day the packaging still looks great, but there are house rats in the palm trees. What was kooky is dangerous; what was whim is weird. Beverly Hills is broke from junkbond failures and the cost of financing the new vainglorious Civic Center. There are boarded storefronts on Rodeo Drive and a commercial vacancy rate of 25 percent. In the Inland Empire's San Bernardino glut capital, the storefront vacancy rate is 33 percent.

In small towns, Waterford, Fulsom, and Lake Elsinor, political gamesmen sold tax-free, pie-in-the-sky municipal bonds to pay for anticipated infrastructure expansion; now they have defaults and depression. In Windsor, two people were run down and killed because curbs cost an unavailable $30 million. The brochures promise "country living" (the renderings always show green Edens), but curbless, dusty, cowboy-movie sets are unexpectedly and overly authentic.

By the year 2010, there will be water shortages nine years out of ten; it is predicted that the twenty-first century will be a "permanent drought." In California, being told that there is no more water is like being told you are going to die; until it happens you hope that God or gold will save you. Politicians are promoting two new aqueducts, each one thousand miles long, to bring water from the wet Pacific Northwest for $1000 an acre-foot, despite the violent protests of Canada's conservationists. We have to figure out how to desalinate the Pacific.

Under the mists of their primeval rain forests, people in the Pacific Northwest see any evidence of visual, economic, and chemical pollution as something that blew in from California.

Bumper stickers say "Don't Californicate Oregon"; GOBK2LA license plates abound; "riplas" (rich invading people from Los Angeles) are not welcomed. Formerly, knocking L.A. was tinged with envy: now it's "Los Angelization: 1) The process in which rapid population growth, uncontrolled development, increasing congestion, rampant crime and environmental damage combine to make other cities in the Western U.S. resemble Los Angeles; 2) A descent into urban hell" (Jordan Bonfante).

Every myth has its own landscape, but the myth of California has been packaged and sold everywhere. The recurrent failure of the real thing only promotes its continuing success as an export. California, brilliant with cosmetics and biotechnology, has painted and packaged its playgrounds, and successfully sold them to a world waiting eagerly to buy new games.

California, originally a refuge from history, is now making fake historic buildings, and real history. Thanks to media and satellite transmissions that defy any boundaries, slick discs, hot tapes, *The Streets of San Francisco*, and *LA Law*, California appears a "land of mystery," mysticism, and light. When you flick on the TV you are never sure if you turned in to an instantaneous revolution or a relevant soap. Landscapes look the same whether we are fighting war games in the Mohave, "freeing" Kuwait on CNN, or playing Nintendo games in the local arcade: there are red mountains on the horizon, white deserts leading straight for them, and everybody zooming to blue skies. Surveys of Russian youths show they prefer California's color to class struggles. Eastern revolutionaries, seduced by free-wheeling consumer hyper-capitalism, announce: "We want to wake up one day and suddenly find we are living in California, where we don't have to stop at red lights" (Emil Ilean, Romanian, age thirty, 1990). Commodities are more fun than Communism.

France, always up on the latest trends, loves and hates L.A./La Défense landscapes: futuristic glass towers, shopping arcades, neon walls, plastic plazas, swooping off-ramps and McDonalds. At the Euro Disney Resort in Marne-La-Vallée, five thousand acres of venerable agrarian settlement have been metamorphosed into an instant LandEscaped playland, a copy of a fake copying a fake, the world as an amusement park, an instant "state of mind" (the developers). The roller-coaster ride with Gold Rush motifs is like a logo of California. A 138-acre Wild West Davy Crockett Campground, with 181 campsites, and parking for 440 RVs, represents roughing-it in the wilderness. "Hundreds of plastic trees are watered to remove dirt from the painted green leaves." It is Manifest Destiny without having to leave France; CaliPorniLand for a price that's less than a plane ticket; D-Day II, a second invasion of the cowboys; Californication for fun and profit.

Disneyworld in Orlando is further California "imagineering" of particular local landscapes (this time of the Florida swamps), into formula International Style theme parks. Everything is clean, safe, uniform, newly painted, and plastic. Even Cape Canaveral looks like a *Star Wars* (1977) rocket ride. Universal and Disney studios have built "Hollywood-East" at Orlando where people can pretend to be Hollywood extras with real actors pretending to make movies on pretend Hollywood movie sets. "When you're in Disney, you have the hope that things can get better . . . hope for a better place, which is of course heaven" (Tammy Faye Baker). Maybe when there are enough Disneylands covering the earth people will go to them, instead of to California. When Anaheim is out of fashion, Californians can pursue new landscapes or even luxuriate in a grandeur of decline.

California as Caprice: sudden whim,
                      style,
                      upside-down
                      with hair
                      standing on end.

Asians sailed east to the "Isles of the Immortals," to "Where the sun rises/In the land of Fu Sang/Seeking fame and riches," long before Europeans rushed west to find paradise.

Since the Ice Age, Asians searching for golden opportunities have been migrating over the landbridge connecting Asia with the Pacific Coast. "In the year of Yung yuan [A.D. 499] a priest by the name of Hui Shen [sailed east to] the Kingdom of Fusang [California] that was 20,000 li [seven thousand miles] east of China" (Great Chinese Encyclopedia, A.D. 502–556).

The Spaniards had accepted the Chinese, (one of the founding fathers of Los Angeles was Antonio Rodriguez, a Chinese settler from Mexico) but the "blue-eyed barbarians" despised them for not being the right color. Is there some reason that white is the Chinese color for mourning? Gold is their color for prosperity. They called California Gold Mountain, and rushed there only to be insulted, excluded, exploited, and feared as the "yellow peril." With patience and muscle, they dug the tunnels and laid the tracks for the railways over the Sierras. They built the bridges and levees that reclaimed the Sacramento and San Joaquin marshlands and tule swamps into the land-rich Delta. They transformed the Central Valley into an agrarian garden. They made California into that garden of the world that the myths had cunningly predicted.

Chinese farmers knew the potential of plants that Yankee farmers saw only as weeds. Every spring the Salinas Valley, from the Pacific inland to Pasa Robles, was yellow with the mustard plants of the Franciscans which had grown wild. The Chinese knew the value of mustard seeds for making cooking oil. One spring, about 1862, an enterprising Chinese gentlemen, called Jim by the white farmers, approached these farmers and volunteered to remove the yellow nuisance from their fields in exchange for the mustard seeds. They agreed. Jim went to San Francisco, contracted a crew of his countrymen, and together they cut down the mustard, removed the seeds, sold some to pay wages, and stored the rest. That year there was a mustard crop failure in Europe and South Africa; merchants scoured the world for mustard seeds. A French mustard broker located Jim in California and paid him thirty-five thousand dollars for his yellow mustard-turned-to-gold.

The Japanese sailed later to the land where the sun rose golden.

"Huge dreams of fortune/Go with me to foreign lands,/Across the ocean."
"Deserts to farmlands/Japanese-American/Page of History. (Kazuo Ito)

Aware of the racist hysteria in paradise, the Japanese relied on ethnic solidarity, enterprise, and their traditional knowledge of intensive farming. Their entry into the California landscape was timely; by the 1890s, irrigation projects and the invention of the refrigerator car allowed a shift from fields of wheat to more lucrative fields of green. They planted grids of fruit orchards, furrows of vegetables, and strawberries in abundance, until even marginal lands in the San Joaquin, Sacramento, and Imperial valleys (as well as everybody's private gardens) looked like Eastern Europe.

Japanese perseverance grows gold in California. Japanese capital is currently buying California from Californians addicted to quick Tokyo investment fixes. They have bought into our most mythic icons: Hollywood and Yosemite. Sony purchased Columbia Pictures, and Matsushita bought MCA, which gave them the Camp Curry concessions in Yosemite Valley. BUY AMERICA t-shirts abound.

For the Japanese, the green grasses of paradise are our golf courses. Golf courses have replaced the bonsai as miniature substitutes for nature. Access to a golf course through the purchase of a million-dollar home is being promoted to the "new Japanese immigrants," just as backyard swimming pools were once targeted to Midwesterners. When the Japanese bought a half interest in the exclusive Riviera Country Club, they were welcomed as investors, not members; since buying the Pebble Beach Company they have been trying to initiate a $750 million membership fee guaranteed to turn the famed green on the Pacific into an exclusive Japanese club.

The "Nipponization" of California has been visually low-key (since they have been planting the landscape all along). Japanese brag that when they migrate here they become 200 percent Californian. Their developments (they own one-third of L.A.'s Gold Coast) have accordingly decorated the landscape with more emerald mirror-glass towers reflected in more greenback pools of water in more plazas with palms in planted boxes over underground parking. The Japanese are eminently adept at the lucrative cross-fertilization between real estate and High Style: high finance is financing High Art. Schuma Investments, which owns more than one billion dollars worth of prime L.A. property, offered to pay for a Statue of Liberty for Los Angeles; this landmark may materialize as a deconstructivist steel (mushroom cloud) floating over the Hollywood Freeway next to Civic Center.

The Pacific Coast has become the Asia Minor of the Pacific Rim to immigrants and entrepreneurs from Japan, Hong Kong, the Philippines, Taiwan, Korea, and Singapore and refugees from the People's Republic of China, Thailand, Vietnam, and Southeast Asia. The Chinese come with flight capital from nervous Hong Kong; the Japanese with trade-generated super-yen. One out of ten Californians is now Asian. Under the Immigration Act of 1990 about ten thousand green cards a year will be given to immigrants with enough "off-shore" capital to create "new commercial enterprises" employing at least ten U.S. citizens. Under this arrangement, the price of a green card can be as high as three million dollars.

For the golden people, Asians and Hispanics, California still looks like paradise.

The Asians who once worked the land are now buying it; the Mexicans who briefly owned it are now working it.

From 1821 to 1848, the Mexicans owned California, tenuously. The 1848 Treaty of Guadalupe Hidalgo supposedly guaranteed property rights to the Mexican Californios. That was the moment, before Yankee arrogance and Gold Rush propaganda destroyed the Mexican culture in California, when accommodation might have shaped the landscape into a georgic Eden of independent homesteads, rather than a grandiose extravaganza of corporate holdings. The Mission Era had ended earlier, but the mission gardens, overgrown, had survived. Acquisitive green-eyed travelers appreciated the aqueducts and alamedas lined with pepper trees, the ceremonial palms, the orchards of oranges, olives, figs, and dates; the fences of prickly pear, vineyards and herbs, the pomegranates, nasturtiums, calla lilies, and roses growing wild. By 1851 Yankee lawyers devised ways to circumvent the inconvenient Treaty; Yankees had Yankee plans for California's cultivation.

In California, agriculture is big business and there is no agri-biz without Mexico's "inexhaustible pool of cheap labor." At harvest time, green card or not, the "golden horde" pours over the border to work the land, to scab on their knees picking strawberries in the Imperial, to breathe pesticides in the Central Valley orchards, to make the Napa Valley vintners richer.

The Hispanics are also creating more colorful, new landscapes. *La Frontera* is a line in the desert, drawn from the Pacific to a spot called Otay Mesa. It is the most heavily traveled border in the world. About forty-three million tourists and migrants each pass through *la frontera* legally; about one million foreigners enter illegally. When they get caught and shipped back, they try again the next day. Along this line the San Ysidro "Light Up the Border" site-specific demonstration occurs. The performance consists of a caravan of "I've-got-mine" Californians in their cars, campers and trucks, parked in phalanx position, facing south toward the Tijuana River. On the other side of the chain-link frontier, Hispanics, mostly Mexican, wait. As the sun sets the Headlight Rally begins. Xenophobic whites switch on their headlights and point hand-held spots straight toward Mexico; the counter demonstrators retaliate with large mirrors to reflect the lights back into California. It is a light show worthy of review by art critics as well as the Border Patrol. The Latinos are lighting up California.

Hispanics (and the homeless) have inherited the abandoned pre-Disneyland downtown streets, parks, and plazas of California. The City of the Angels is Catholic again; San Francisco's Mission District, Sacramento, Stockton, the Valley towns, are alive with people walking on the streets. There are open storefront markets, colored signs for restaurants and auto shops, neon bar signs, Latino festivities, noise, music, gangs, and drugs included. The old movie marquees announce Spanish-language movies, and the palm trees don't look as plastic. Chicano murals are painted on every blank wall, and curb side parks have appeared. Even if the Latino teenagers prefer hanging out in front of Tower Records at the local mall, the tourists come to take the Sunday *paseo* at the plaza.

Without green cards, Hispanics get into California to live in hillside dugouts and camp in RVs and cars near, but out of sight of, the million-dollar homes whose owners hire them to work in their gardens one day and vote to remove the "immigrant blight" the next. With green cards they can plant their own gardens in East L.A., in the Santa Ana barrio, or in overpriced shacks on the wrong side of the San Diego Freeway.

Upwardly mobile Chicanos can move to the San Gabriel Valley tracks. Since the Pomona Freeway slashed a fast track through what was the world's greatest citrus orchard, the valley has grown into a green suburb of golden faces. A quarter of a million Hispanics, with their potential voting power, represent a political threat to the slow-growth whites. The most "white-is-rightists" want a statewide "Elbow Room" initiative to close off the Mexican border.

Despite all the whitewalling, there has been a 90 percent increase in Third World immigration into the Los Angeles area; in San Francisco, white flight has left the San Francisco public schools an 86 percent "ethnic minority" majority. Since 1980 the Hispanic community has grown 70 percent; the Asian community 127 percent. Latinos and Asians are fighting to draw up fair new political remappings of legislative boundaries. In 1991 Asians students outnumbered whites in the freshman class at the University of California in Berkeley. Demographics show that California is already only 57 percent white. The way things are going, by 2003 whites will be the minority in California.

Perhaps California was never destined for the white man, and it would have been better for him, and for the rest of the world, if he had never moved here.

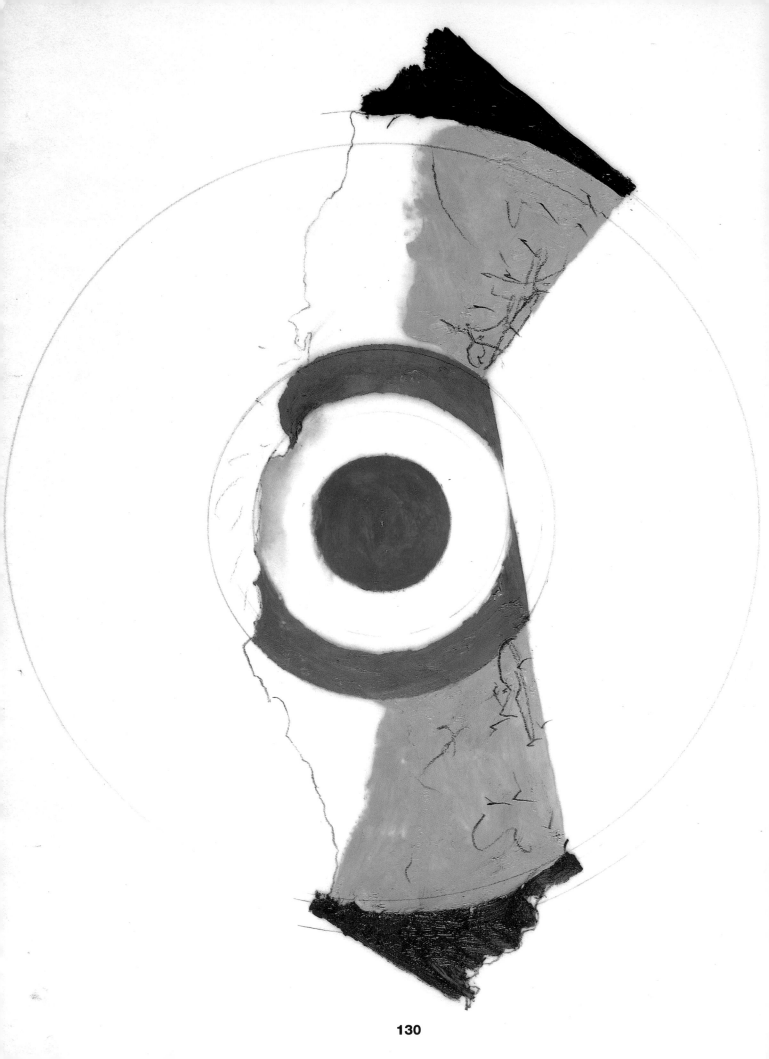

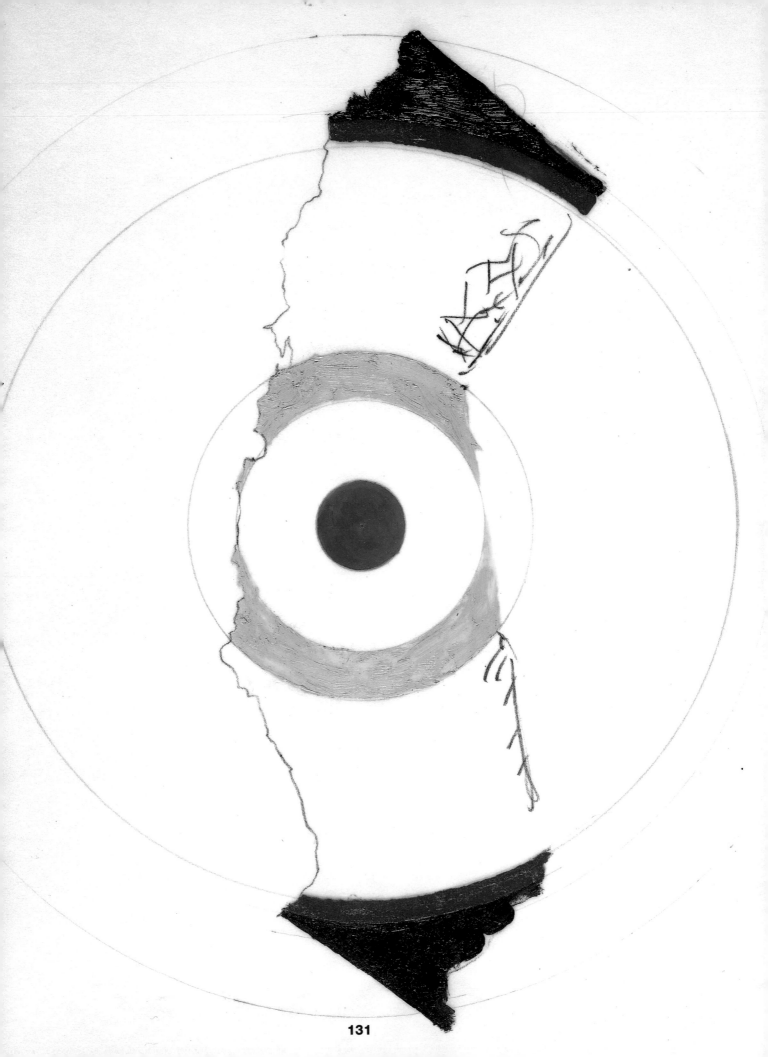

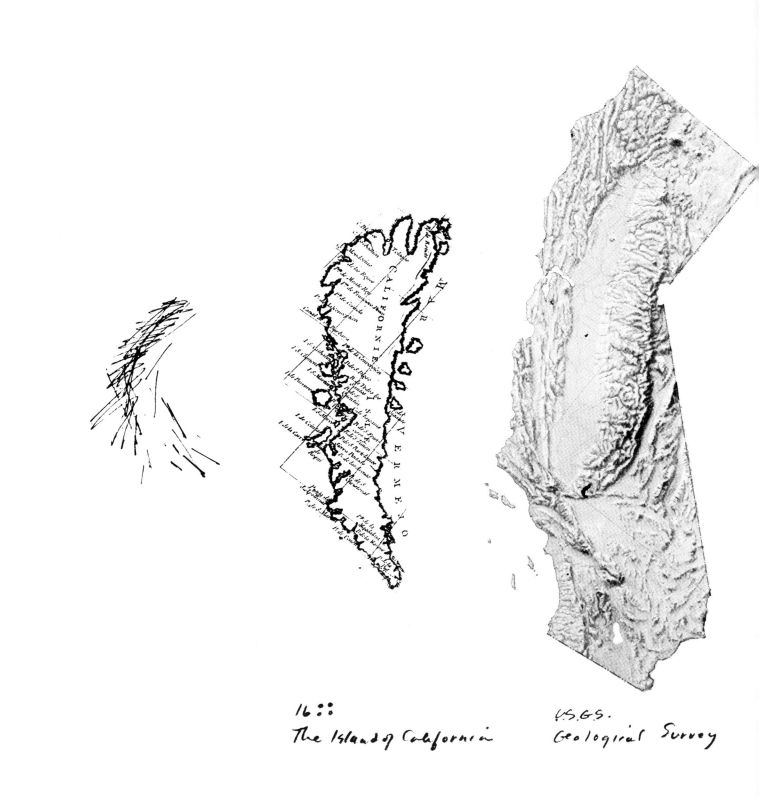

16 ::
The Island of California

U.S.G.S.
Geological Survey

1990

Rand McNally's

California

133

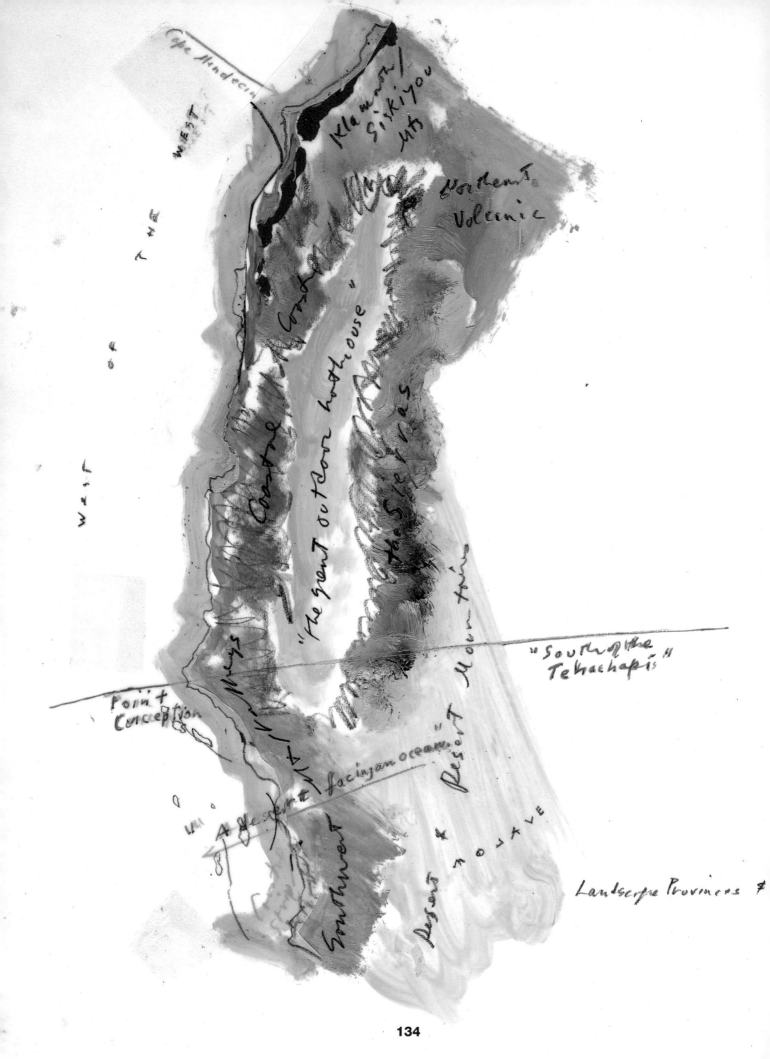

Cape Mindocin

WEST

Klamath/
Siskiyou
Mts

Northern
Volcanic

THE

Coastal

"The great outdoor hothouse"

The Sierras

West OF

"South of the
Tehachapis"

Point
Conception

"A desert facing an ocean"

Southwest

Present Mountain

Desert
MOJAVE

Landscape Provinces †

Major Faults.

For Californians, California is a full-size map of her possibilities. Maps of myths make the invisible visible. Maps are fictions, but there is truth in lies if you tell enough of them, as Lamar Trotti wrote in the screen play for *The Ox-bow Incident* (1943).

In *Dreamtigers*, Jorge Luis Borges tells a tale in which cartographers draw a map of the Empire so detailed that it ends up completely covering the territory. As the Empire declines, the map frays until only a few shreds remain, charming ruins, "in the deserts of the West."

In California, we drew our map quickly, only two hundred years for this first layer that we live in. It was drawn by many people, on many pieces of paper and film, glued together. In California, the map became the Empire. Sometimes someone will look for remains of territory visible through the splices, but Californians are born with a golden resin exuding from their eyes, so that as they go to look for charming ruins between the cracks their magic mending-tape eyes automatically fix over any tears.

For the properly addicted, California is a moviola, a machine we have in the movie business: "a wonderful thing—maybe the *most* wonderful. If you use it right, you can make time go backwards and forwards, faster and slower; you can stop time and stay . . . ; you can cut out the parts you don't like, and the parts you *do* like you can have over and over" (B. J. Farber). Now everyone has to have his VHS-VCR. California is a movie map: infinite images of the landscape, shot, edited, repeated and eliminated, dispersed, multiple, continuous and ephemeral, projected as Cinemascope on screens of air.

Changing landscapes is addictive; flicking over images had become an obsession. On the freeway we move forward while sitting still. Watching TV we sit in one spot and everything is moving too fast to see more than the surface glitter. We float through the freeways and the media, of which we are somehow a part.

Changing lanes and channels, we are no long captive in the garden. Driving ourselves, we are free to speed up, slow down, go backwards and stop. Watching TV we are in a lighted room; we can flick from one plot to another, we can see the stuff outside the screen, outside the frame, and outside the window. We can mix up the stories, skip the commercials, and catch the war news at half-time. We are no longer glued to our seats in the black movie box without windows, at the mercy of the projectionist playing off someone else's linear plot. We can escape confinement; for a Californian, the worst possible prison. Geographic claustrophobia is death. When we push the buttons we can pretend to be the editor. We can zoom back and forth between the sublime and the banal, rushing and choosing incessantly from one crystallized blinking landscape to another. The only rules of the game that remain are traffic signs.

In our "civilization of images" we are deliriously bombarded "by such a quantity of images that we can no longer distinguish direct experience from what we have seen for a few seconds on television" (Italo Calvino).

In California we excel in making images, and we love living in landscapes of images. We move; they move. Each view is a free-floating film of the transparent, the transcending, and the trashy. The myths are real, and they change constantly. We assume the special effects are rigged, which leaves us free to enjoy the spectacle. Each landscape we look at is in front of our eyes and somewhere else at the same time, as ubiquitous as God and TV. We are constantly astonished, naive, and numb. On TV, views change faster than we can focus on them; on the freeway, views rush by fast, blurred, and forgettable. Everything and everybody is overexposed.

No one ever wanted to look at the landscape too closely:
"An evening light is generally the best for all landscapes" (Anthony Trollope, 1862).
"We can double the true beauty of an actual landscape by half closing our eyes as
we look at it. The naked senses sometime see too little—but then always they see
too much" (Edgar Allan Poe, 1844).

In California there is too much light to see. Details are lost in the flashing brightness.
The cautious wear dark glasses. Like any brilliant art, the results are better if you go
fast, if the images aren't finished. If you drive fast enough the view is a blur, but if you
go faster the landscape stands still and you just float through it. *Vertigo* (1958),
superlative and sublime.

Landscapes are the surfaces of the spectacle. In California, where everything
underground is dangerous, complicated, and to be avoided, we have become
proficient at surfaces. We like vistas waiting for something surprising and
entertaining to happen, quickly. Our egocentric eyeballs crave views that are empty
and potential.

Empty space is why everybody came here in the first place. Space itself is spiritual
capital, compensation for the long trip, our manifested destiny. We see the
landscape as a blank canvas stretched, waiting and ready; a blank TV screen,
crackling, before the images appear; empty space, open silence, fluid and free for
brilliant illusions.

In California we crave the glaring walls of sky, the Pacific, the desert, the open road,
and views where it is impossible to see the end. We lust after the luxury of open
space, the luxury that money can still buy in California: vacuous suburbs, dormant
golden fields, wide city streets with elbow room, beach houses with views of nothing
forever. We like to sit in jets thirty-five thousand feet up, surveying mountaintops,
highways, and cities that look like printed throwaways that we are free to throw
away. The wise leave the film out of the camera and take pictures with their eyes.

The best landscapes in California are those that disappear: towers of mirrored glass
reflecting the sun, gold from the sunset, vanishing into the sky; skyscrapers
disappearing up into the fog or smog; the air and clouds in between the buildings;
voids to be filled, vacant lots, idle farmlands, median strips; the false fronts of
franchised enterprises that will be gone tomorrow. There are strip cities and gas
stations, freeways and airports, instant shopping centers and suburbs, landscapes
put up to be torn down for the next opportunity. If we hesitate, an earthquake will
give us a clean slate to start again from the beginning.

California is a fast edited-montage of disrespect and incongruity that fulfills
everybody's insatiable eye hunger, for the moment. We rush so fast into the
vanishing point that everything vanishes. California exists so vividly in everyone's
imagination that it no longer needs geography. We feed everyone's appetite for
entertaining images, and they call us "the myth of the twentieth century." The
landscape is a shining mirage. It shimmers.

California is an agreed-upon illusion. The only reason anyone believes it is that
everyone does. The artificial landscapes are genuine, only made of different stuff,
and Californians are sinfully successful with synthetic effects. We use them to make
disposable views and longshots, slashes of the possible, drawn up and down the
map at the end of the world that is changing, by chance just beginning.

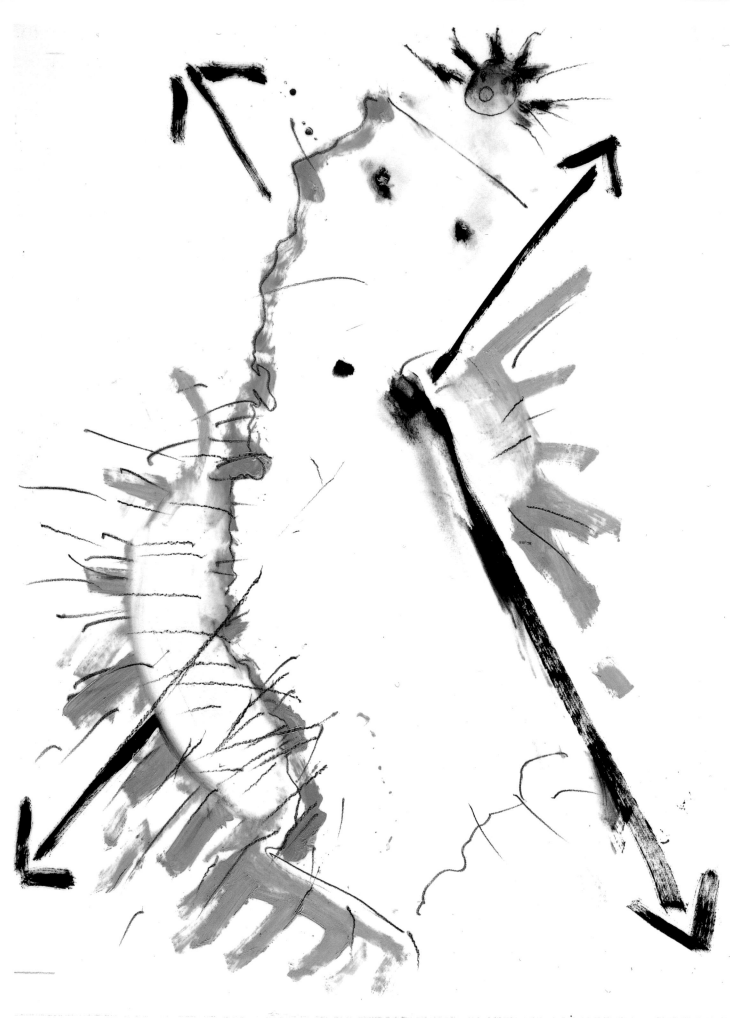

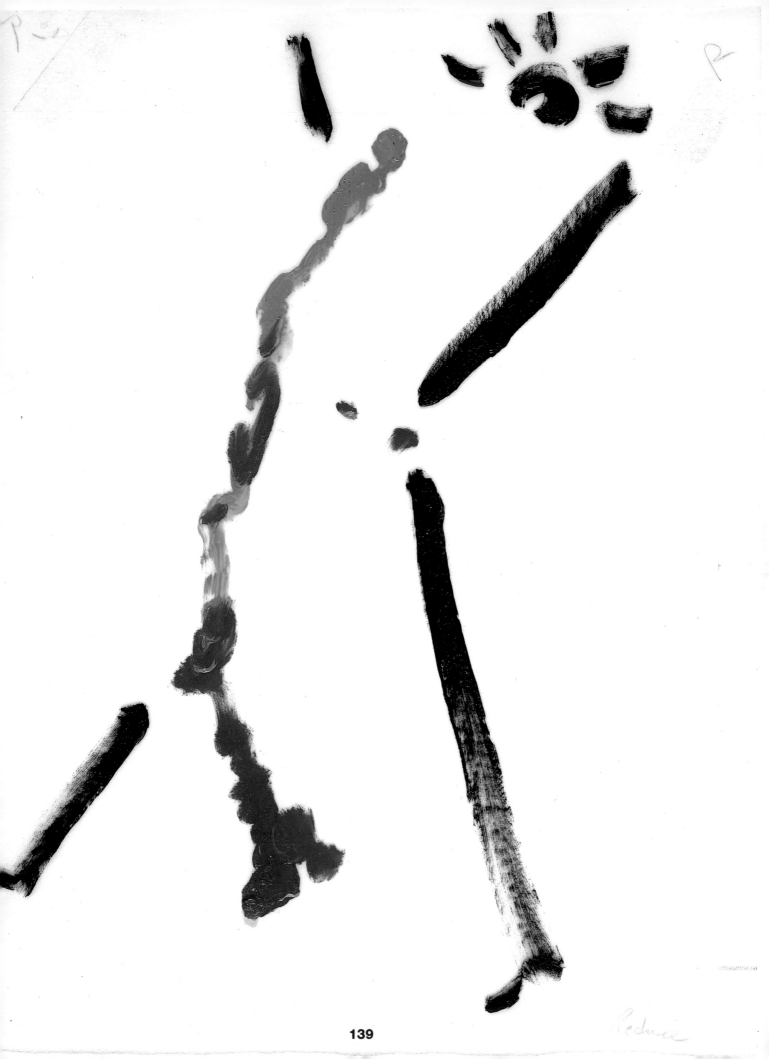

# Bibliography

I gratefully acknowledge the following sources for research material and quotes in *Good Mourning America*.

## The Island of California

Hale, Edward Everett
*The Queen of California.* San Francisco: Colt Press, 1945. This book contains translations of passages from Garcia Ordóñez de Montalvo, *Las sergas de Esplandian* (1510).

Leighly, John
*California as an Island.* San Francisco: The Book Club of California, 1972.

Purvis, Andrew
"The Antarctic Connection." *Time,* 8 April 1991.

## NATURE

Anderson, Nancy K., and Linda S. Ferber
*Albert Bierstadt: Art and Enterprise.* Brooklyn: The Brooklyn Museum, 1991.

Barich, Bill
"Acts of Attention." In *Picturing California.* San Francisco: Chronicle Books, 1989.

Barth, Gunther
*Fleeting Moments.* New York: Oxford University Press, 1990.

Barthes, Roland
*The Responsibility of Forms.* Berkeley: University of California Press, 1985.

Baudrillard, Jean
*America.* London and New York: Verso, 1988.

*Revenge of the Crystal.* Sidney: Pluto Press, 1990.

Buell, L.
"American Pastoral Ideology," *American Literary History* 1, no. 1 (Spring 1989).

Burke, Edmund
*A Philosophical Enquiry into the Origin of our Ideas of the Sublime and the Beautiful,* part 2, sec. 1. P.F. Collier & Son, New York, 1937.

Fuller, Peter
"The Geography of Mother Nature." In "Earthbound," by Rebecca Solnit, unpublished.

Gilmore, Michael T.
*American Romanticism and the Marketplace.* Chicago: University of Chicago Press, 1985.

Ginsberg, Allen
"A Supermarket in California." Quoted in *West of the West,* by Leonard Michaels, David Reid, and Raquel Scheer. San Francisco: North Point Press, 1989.

Hughes, Robert
"How the West was Spun." *Time,* 13 May 1991.

Hyde, Anne Farrer
*An American Vision: Far Western Landscape and National Culture, 1820–1920.* New York; New York University Press, 1990.

Kahn, et al.
"One Day of Mall Hopping." *The Chronicle,* 10 June 1991.

King, Clarence
"Mount Whitney." Quoted in *West of the West,* by Michaels, Reid, and Scherr. San Francisco: North Point Press, 1989.

Lovejoy, Arthur O.
"The Need to Distinguish Romanticisms." In *Essays in the History of Ideas.* Baltimore: Johns Hopkins University Press, 1948.

Marx, Leo
*The Machine in the Garden.* New York: Oxford University Press, 1964.

Nash, Roberick Frazier
*The Rights of Nature.* Madison: Wisconsin University Press, 1989.

Smith, Henry Nash
*Virgin Land.* Cambridge: Harvard University Press, 1950.

Starr, Kevin
*Americans and the California Dream.* New York: Oxford University Press, 1973.

*Inventing the Dream.* New York: Oxford University Press, 1985.

*Material Dreams.* New York: Oxford University Press, 1990.

Thoreau, Henry David
*The Journal of Henry David Thoreau.* 1906. Dover 1962 [publisher], 1949.

*Walden.* 1854. Reprint. Princeton: Princeton University Press, 1971.

Whitman, Walt
*Leaves of Grass.* 1855. Reprint. New York: Penguin, 1959.

*Drum-Taps.* New York: 1865.

Worster, Donald
*Nature's Economy.* Cambridge: Cambridge University Press, 1977.

Wyatt, David
*The Fall into Eden.* Cambridge: Cambridge University Press, 1983.

## GARDENS

Calvino, Italo
*Mr. Palomar.* New York: Harcourt Brace Jovanovich, 1985.

*Six Memos for the Next Millennium.* Cambridge: Harvard University Press, 1988.

Charyn, Jerome
*Movieland: Hollywood and the Great American Dream Culture.* New York: Putnam, 1989.

Craig, Lois
"Suburbs." In *Design Quarterly* 132. Minneapolis: Walker Art Center, 1986.

Davis, Mike
*City of Quartz.* London and New York: Verso, 1990.

Frampton, Kenneth
"Eisenman Revisited: Running Interference." *A+U,* 1988.

Helphand, Kenneth
"Landscape Films." *Landscape Journal* 5, no. 1 (1988).

"Battlefields & Dreamfields." In *Oregon Humanities.*

Miller, Naomi
"Paradise Revisited: Medieval Garden Fountains." In *Medieval Gardens.* Washington, D.C.: Dumbarton Oaks Research Library and Collection, 1986.

Reisner, Marc
*Cadillac Desert.* New York: Penguin, 1987.

Strang, Gary
"Infrastructure as Landscape." Unpublished.

Wollen, Peter
*Signs & Meanings in the Cinema.* Indiana University Press, 1972.

Woods, Michael
"America in the Movies." In *West of the West,* by Michaels, Reid, and Scherr. San Francisco: North Point Press, 1989.

## LANDSCAPÉS

Baudrillard, Jean
*Selected Writings.* Palo Alto,: Stanford University Press, 1988.

Boas, Nancy
*The Society of Six.* San Francisco: Bedford Arts, 1988.

Bonfante, Jordan
"Everybody's Fall Guy." *Time,* 10 June 1991.

Borges, Jorge Luis
*Dreamtigers.* Austin: University of Texas Press, 1989.

Brodsky, David
*L.A. Freeway.* Berkeley: University of California Press, 1981.

Bukowski, Charles
*Hollywood.* Santa Rosa, Calif.: Black Sparrow Press, 1989.

Davis, Mike
*City of Quartz.* London and New York: Verso, 1990.

Didion, Joan
"Notes from a Native Daughter." In *Slouching Towards Bethlehem.* New York: Touchstone, 1979.

"Letter from Los Angeles." *The New Yorker,* 4 September 1989.

Feyerabend, Paul
"Cultural Pluralism or or Brave New Monotony." *Precis* 6 (1985).

Hill, Mary
*California Landscape.* Berkeley: University of California Press, 1984.

Le Guin, Ursula K.
"A Non-Euclidean View of California." In "Earthbound." unpublished.

Lippard, Lucy R.
*Mixed Blessings.* New York: Pantheon, 1990.

Lydon, Sandy
*Chinese Gold.* Capitola Book Company, 1985.

Milosz, Czeslaw
"The Events in California." In *West of the West,* by Michaels, Reid, and Scherr. San Francisco: North Point Press, 1989.

Painton, Pricilla
"Fantasy's Reality." *Time,* 27 May 1991.

Smilgis, Martha
"Hollywood Goes to Heaven." *Time,* 3 June 1991.

Soja, Edward W.
*Postmodern Geographics.* London: Verso, 1990.

Steiner, Stan.
*FuSang: The Chinese Who Built America.* New York: Harper & Row, 1979.

Varnedoe, Kirk, and Adam Gopnick
*High & Low: Modern Art & Popular Culture.* New York: Museum of Modern Art, 1991.

Wolfert, Lee
"This Art's for You" *L.A. Style* (June 1990).

# Credits

12–13
*Novus Planiglobii Terrestri*
*per Utrumque Polum Conspectus,*
Joan Blaeu-Gerard Valck (ca. 1695),
The Bancroft Library,
University of California,
Berkeley, California.

16
*Globe Terres,,*
Pierre du Val (2), Paris, 1666,
The Bancroft Library,
University of California,
Berkeley, California.

17
Projected maps from
An Album of Map Projectioms,
U.S. Geological Survey Professional Paper,
1453.

28
*Yosemite Valley, 1868,*
Albert Bierstadt,
The Oakland Musem,
Oakland, California.

29
California Museum of Photography,
Raoul Gradrohl Collection,
University of California, Riverside.

32
Uncle Sam,
Orange Box Label (ca. 1898),
Linda MacKie Collection,
Riverside Navel Orange Co.

56
*Sunrise, Yosemite Valley,*
Albert Bierstadt,
Amon Carter Museum,
Fort Worth, Texas.